PRAISE FOR BOYD CLEWIS AND
THROUGH THE FIREWALL

"Boyd is an incredibly talented cybersecurity leader, and to have read his backstory and learn of how he overcame challenges that should have grounded him, left me super inspired. More so, this book has an actionable way of taking Boyd's life lessons and empowering you to review your life and make better decisions going forward. I'll highly recommend this book to not just young people but also to everyone looking for a will and way to reinvent their lives and rewrite their stories."

—CONFIDENCE STAVELEY
Africa's most celebrated female cybersecurity leader, talent developer, global speaker and inclusion advocate

"Boyd is transforming lives simply by telling the stories from his own life experiences, and it is something special. *Through the Firewall: The Alchemy of Turning Crisis into Opportunity* allows you to open your eyes to opportunities and manifest your destiny. To never give up. This book can serve as a strong, silent mentor. It has so far for me. It maintains productive values and reminds you to never give up hope. I strongly believe that people like Boyd can change the course of this world just by telling their story. You will be inspired to push harder and dig deeper in everything you do. Propel yourself to reach your full and true potential. This book also serves as a reminder that the path to courage and success arrives through embracing pain and fear, not by avoiding them. *Through the Firewall* has the ability to better the mind, but most importantly, Boyd teaches you how."

—EVAN ANDERSON
Anchor/reporter, NBC5 Today, Dallas-Fort Worth

"*Through the Firewall*, by Boyd Clewis, is an inspiring and powerful story of a young man overcoming obstacles to reach his goals.

Boyd shares his experiences in a way that resonates with readers, from financial struggles and academic pressure to his newfound ambition. *Through the Firewall* emphasizes the value of hard work, resilience, and perseverance in achieving success. It is a must-read for anyone wanting to find inspiration and strength in their own life journey, as well as anyone needing to be reminded of their own worth and potential, regardless of where their journey started. Boyd's story will encourage readers to never give up on their dreams, no matter how seemingly insurmountable the challenge."

—RAESHAWN M. CANNON
Sister, best-selling author, 20 Beautiful Women

"When you're establishing a career, and everything in life seems to be going wrong, the one thing you need is a plan. *Through the Firewall* delivers a true-to-life story of overcoming life's obstacles and achieving one's goals."

—NIR EYAL
Best-selling author, Hooked; Indistractable

THROUGH THE FIREWALL

THE ALCHEMY OF TURNING
CRISIS INTO **OPPORTUNITY**

THROUGH THE
FIREWALL

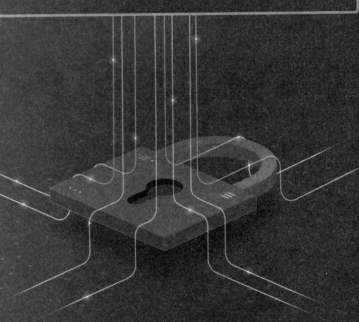

BOYD CLEWIS

Forbes | Books

Published by Forbes Books, Charleston, South Carolina.
Member of Advantage Media.

Forbes Books is a registered trademark, and the Forbes Books colophon is a trademark of Forbes Media, LLC.

Printed in the United States of America.

10 9 8 7 6 5 4 3 2 1

ISBN: 979-8-88750-180-2 (Hardcover)
ISBN: 979-8-88750-181-9 (eBook)

LCCN: 2022923452

Book design by Analisa Smith.

Since 1917, Forbes has remained steadfast in its mission to serve as the defining voice of entrepreneurial capitalism. Forbes Books, launched in 2016 through a partnership with Advantage Media, furthers that aim by helping business and thought leaders bring their stories, passion, and knowledge to the forefront in custom books. Opinions expressed by Forbes Books authors are their own. To be considered for publication, please visit books.Forbes.com.

To my wife, Tiana B. Clewis, because I wouldn't be the man I am without her support. To my family for never giving up on me. To Rob Hemsley and D. J. Searcy for showing me the Plano way. And to my four children for giving me a reason to push through tough times.

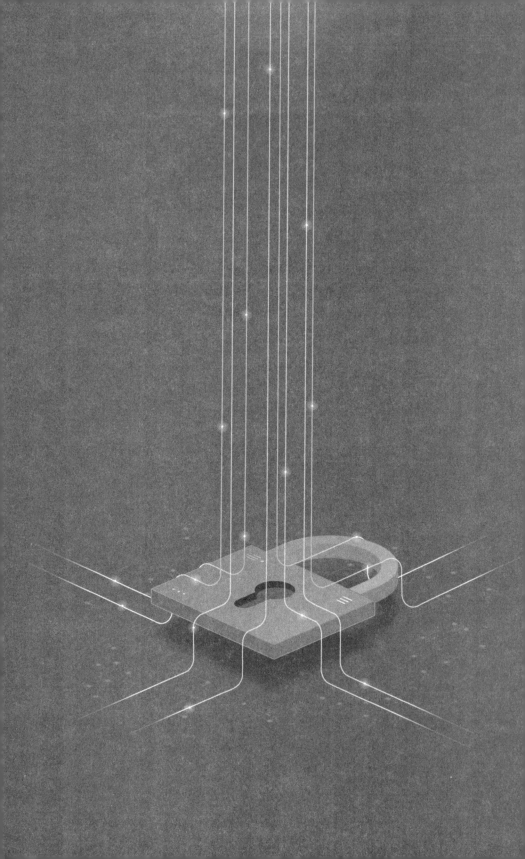

CONTENTS

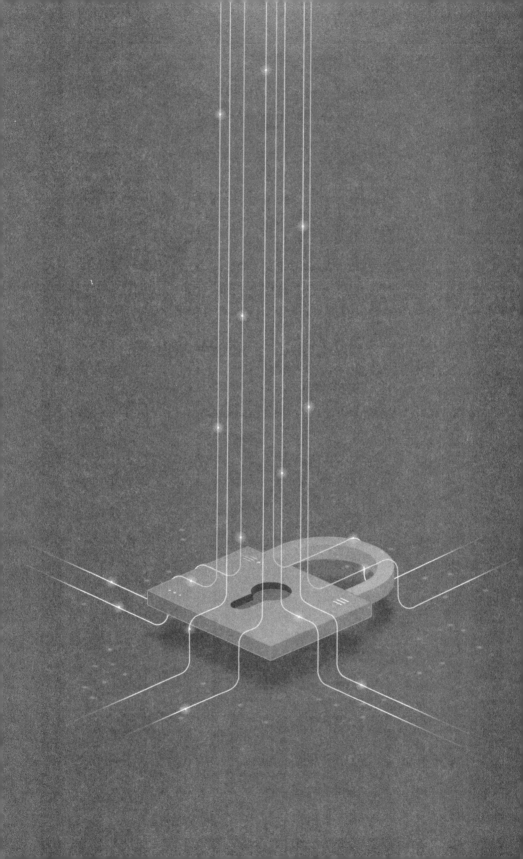

FOREWORD

Life can be messy.

And when Boyd and I began dating in 2014, *messy* was the perfect word to describe his life. He was in the middle of a contentious divorce with his first wife that had shocked some of us at church. They'd thrown a fabulous Christmas party just a few months before, and no one suspected that their marriage would be one of the 40 percent that end in divorce. To this day, Facebook periodically shows us pictures of that party.

Messy.

Like 49 percent of young black men, he was walking through life with an arrest record that would disqualify him from many types of positions.[1] In fact, one of those arrests had happened weeks before our first date. Helping him get a good lawyer was one of the weirdest things I ever did for him as a girlfriend.

Messy.

He had been living with an undiagnosed mental health issue that had shaped his life and decisions in ways he wouldn't know until

---

1   "Study: Nearly Half of Black Males, 40 Percent of White Males Arrested by 23," UMD College of Behavioral & Social Sciences, https://bsos.umd.edu/featured-content/study-nearly-half-black-males.

much later. It wouldn't be until our own marriage was in peril that he learned that he was among only 2.8 percent of adults in the United States living with this issue.[2]

Messy.

As for his education, let's say that his college transcript had more incompletes on it than actual grades. Like 65 percent of low-income students, he'd left with no degree but plenty of debt. For a while, it looked like the paycheck-to-paycheck lifestyle with more debt than assets would be inevitable.

I could easily keep going, but you get the point: life can be messy. However, a messy life doesn't also have to mean untapped potential and unfulfilled dreams. While Boyd's life was definitely messy and downright chaotic at times, he was always moving forward. Mistakes were made and opportunities were missed, but he never allowed those messy statistics to turn into a death sentence for his future.

As you read through this book, you'll learn how Boyd turned his mess into the awe-inspiring legacy that he continues to build each and every day. You'll see the steps that he took on his journey to defy the odds in his professional and personal life. You'll hear the thought process behind his actions—some that slowed him down and others that propelled him forward. You'll witness the moments that could have broken him, but instead, showed Boyd himself. These led to Boyd owning his mistakes and growing into the husband, father, minister, and moneymaking leader that he is today.

You'll also realize that you can do the same.

Throughout this book, we tried to pick out key lessons, moments, and strategies that pushed Boyd in the right direction. When you come across these points, take a moment to consider how those same

---

2   "Bipolar Disorder," National Institute of Mental Health, https://www.nimh.nih.gov/health/statistics/bipolar-disorder.

things might be relevant to your own life, and with that knowledge, create a plan to help yourself overcome obstacles and move toward the future you desire for yourself.

The things we've highlighted here aren't the only golden nuggets in this book. While you're reading, something buried in the middle of a chapter may kick you square in the chest. As Boyd likes to say in his sermons, "Be sure to take notes, because I may say something profound and not remember it later."

We encourage you to highlight, underline, and flag pages throughout this book as you see fit. We won't be offended if we see you with a multicolored, dog-eared copy. Frankly, it would be a signal that you're really diving into these lessons, just as we hope. When we see this kind of engagement with the students at our academy, we know success is bound to be coming their way—it shows that they're likely to act on their new knowledge.

Consider this book the defining moment when your messy past can no longer stop you from building the type of career and future you've always dreamed about. Yes, the journey will be rough at times. The path may be fraught with missteps and frustrations. But the path is still there, waiting to take you to your vision of success.

Just as Boyd found his path, you can find yours too—if you allow yourself to embrace what's in this book. You just have to take the time to let the knowledge sink in and then put it to work.

Now, without further ado, let's jump into my husband's story, so that you can use his journey as a cheat sheet for your own. Happy reading!

Tiana B. Clewis
Wife of Boyd Clewis | President of Baxter Clewis, LLC

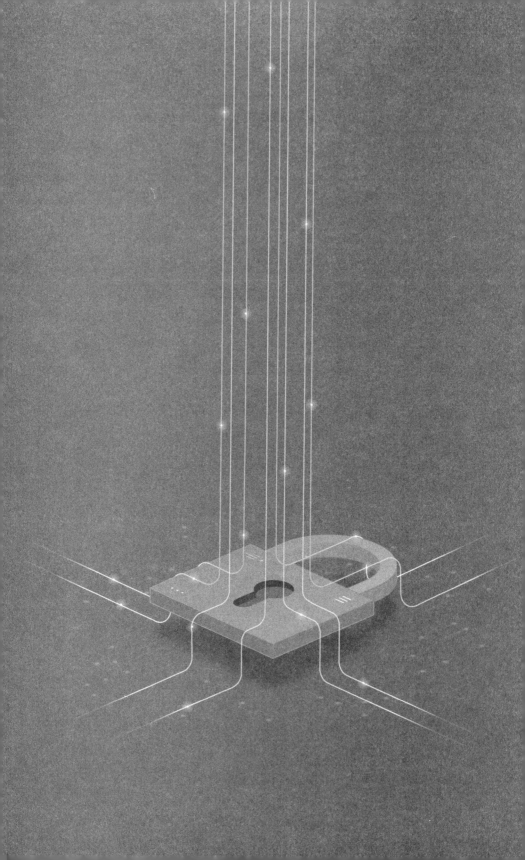

CHAPTER 1

Born Dead

On July 16, 1987, at 1:56 a.m., I was born dead.

My mom went in for emergency labor as my heart rate kept dropping and dropping. When the doctors did an ultrasound, they discovered that my umbilical cord was unusually long, wrapped around my neck three times, and tied in a knot. Every time my mom had a contraction, it would choke me. They rushed her into surgery for an emergency C-section, and by the time they got me out, I was discolored from not breathing. Miraculously, the doctors managed to resuscitate me. I was my mom's third kid, and she never had issues giving birth to my siblings. She still says with all that trouble getting here, there must have been something special about me.

I don't have a lot of memories from my earliest years, but I do know that I was a terrible child. I mean, *terrible*. I misbehaved like you would not believe. I acted out in class, flipped desks, blurted things out, put my hood up and fell asleep at my desk, generally disregarded teachers, got up and walked around when I wasn't supposed to ... the works. I also wasn't the most studious person—never have been. Most of all, it was easier to be a distraction than dealing with the fact that I didn't see myself as a smart guy.

I got in enough trouble that they sent me to an alternative school in third grade—for correction, if you will. Some alternative schools are great, but mine was not one of them. They didn't have a school bus, so my dad had to hire a transportation service to pick me up and drop me off. We were broke, so he was not pleased. We sat in cubicles with our faces to the wall, with dividers between each person. No recess, no cafeteria, no contact with anybody. I silently ate the same peanut butter and jelly sandwich and bag of chips every day. But with no way to get in trouble there, I only had to stay for six weeks. Time served.

When I got back to my previous school, my grades and behavior were still so bad that the teachers recommended a test to see if I had some sort of mental disability. I saw a psychologist, who tested my IQ. They came back with the results like, "This kid is smart! It's probably just not being channeled in the right way." My parents weren't exactly surprised. They knew I wasn't dumb. Like a lot of kids at the time, they put me on Adderall for a couple of years. That helped make me less of a distraction in class, but I still wasn't totally comprehending things. To this day, I still get distracted easily. I just zone out. Someone can be talking to me, and I'm just not there. My wife calls it my "nothing box."

When my parents were together, we lived in Keller, a decent area north of Fort Worth. After school, I was always Rollerblading. I would get lost for hours skating through the nice neighborhoods nearby, imagining what it would be like to live in the huge houses, wondering what the people in them did for a living. I always told my friends:

when I grow up, I'm gonna be *rich*. I've believed it since I was young, wholeheartedly, and regardless of what other people thought or felt about me. I just knew it.

In fifth grade, my parents got divorced. It was like a jump cut. Our two-income household went to two one-income households. Our church had been giving us cheap rent on the big house we'd been living in, and now we had to move out. My brother and I had to help my dad refurbish everything before we left.

We moved to the Town Suites Motel in Arlington. I can still remember the first day we moved in. The Krispy Kreme across the street was giving away free doughnuts. My dad and brother slept in the bed, and I put two chairs together and slept on those. After a month of that, the three of us moved into my aunt's house for the summer. We all shared her second bedroom, and I slept on the floor.

My dad used to make decent money driving garbage trucks to the dump but was laid off after crushing his knee on the job. After that, my dad, my brother, and I started to go to construction sites at night, looking through the dumpsters for scrap metal to sell. Some nights we'd get up at three o'clock in the morning to provide janitorial services at different businesses. This did not help my situation at school.

One day my dad came home and introduced us to his new girlfriend, Janice, and the next thing you know, we're moving in with her. It wasn't a big house, but it was nice and in a decent neighborhood. It had three bedrooms, and I shared a room with my brother. This was an improvement—I wasn't sleeping on chairs or the floor.

Soon, I learned from a card in the mail that I failed sixth grade. Fortunately, we moved again, so I transferred to *another* school and threw the card away. At the next school, they just put me in the seventh grade with everyone else. Of all these transitions, this is the one that really started to shape the person I'd become. I went from mostly white schools to mostly black. It was a *big* difference, and a complete culture shock.

When I finally started talking, all the guys were calling me "white boy" because I didn't talk like them. Their euphemisms and slang were totally foreign to me.

I'm sitting at my desk and this guy next to me says he's "finna to go to the bathroom."

"What does that even mean?"

"You know, I'm fixing to go do something. I'm about to go do something."

"Why didn't you just say, 'I'm about to go?'"

To this day, *finna* still doesn't feel right coming out of my mouth. The other thing was *kai*. "Kai borrow a pencil? Kai go to the bathroom?" I'm thinking, *Who's Kai? And how am I supposed to make it here?*

It was also immediately clear that what was important to my classmates was not important to me. These people were *fashionable*. Nice clothes, Air Jordans, all that good stuff. Where I'm from, I never thought about things like that. I was busy wearing JNCOs and Rollerblading. Our financial situation was still really bad, so I didn't have new school clothes. The guys in my class quickly got to talking about my clothes and shoes. I was showing up wearing stuff that was obviously worn, and kids are cruel. This went on all year.

I had all this upheaval going on at home, still working nights with my dad, getting maybe a few hours of sleep, and trying to make the transition to a new school. I've always been an introvert. Making friends is something I rarely, if ever, consider, mostly because I just changed schools entirely too much.

However, seventh grade was the year when things changed for me academically. I went from the retained failure in sixth grade to an academic standout. One of our teachers, Miss Rose, would toss a Tootsie Roll at anyone who answered a question correctly, and I was catching those things all the time.

I fell in love with science and won the science fair. I still remember the name of the project: "Algae: More or Less." I walked down to the community park, scooped some algae out of the pond, and was cultivating it under the kitchen sink and all over the house, measuring how fast it grew. A year before I was this "dumb" kid who was always getting in trouble, and now suddenly everyone was calling me a nerd.

At the end of that year, all the students had an annual shaving cream fight. People were smacking people with it, throwing it everywhere, and it was a *blast*. Right in the middle of this, I see my dad pull up in the car. Again: We're moving. I was too young to realize it, but he and Janice had been on the outs. Being a Christian man, he didn't like living under the same roof as a woman without being married. In no time he introduced us to his *new* girlfriend, Rosemary, who had been his girlfriend in elementary school. They ended up getting married *the next week*.

At first, it was cool. She was nice to us and had a big house in Fort Worth: four bedrooms, swimming pool, giant trampoline, pool table. I walked in for the first time thinking *This is weird, but it may not be bad?* We had bunk beds, so this was the first time I didn't have to share a bed in I don't know how many years. That whole summer we were having a grand old time jumping off that trampoline into her pool.

Then, somewhere along the line, Rosemary changed. She became the strictest woman I've ever met, and I wasn't accustomed to that kind of thing. She just had this tone that I did not receive well. One day, I was washing the dishes in a way that didn't meet her standards.

She yelled at me, and my reaction was basically, "Hold on. You're not gonna talk to me like that. My *mom* doesn't even talk to me like that." She then went to get a belt and tried to use that to discipline me, and I wasn't having it.

I took the belt from her and got in her face like, "We're *not* doing this."

To which she replied, "And *you're* not gonna disrespect *me* in *my* house."

All the while, my dad's just sitting there, doing nothing. She told me to pack my stuff and leave. I got my things together and put it all in a trash bag, and my dad drove me to my mom's across town.

She and my sister were living in a two-bedroom apartment, so I made my bed on the couch. I'm the youngest, and my sister's the oldest. She didn't go through all the transitions that my brother and I did. Her life was much more streamlined. She never changed schools, and because we have different dads, she always stayed with my mom. She's a brainiac, always went to a special magnet school, and her classmates were the same people for most of her life.

But my mom was still living in the hood—I'll just call it what it is. She was a teacher's aide and couldn't afford to live anywhere nicer. There were people sitting on their stoops smoking weed up and down the block—fairly normal now, but still pretty taboo back then.

Break-ins were not uncommon. My brother and I were home alone one day, and someone just kept knocking on the door. When we didn't answer, the guy kicked in the door. My brother and I ran and hid in the closet. When he pulled it open, my brother put his arm around me, told the guy to take what he wanted, and to leave us alone. My mom had a fancy cordless phone, so the robber just ripped that out of the wall and fled.

At my mom's, I fortunately didn't have to be a night-shift janitor or search for scrap metal in the dark. But I *did* end up having to change schools. Again. But this time, it was good. This school was predominantly Hispanic. There were uniforms, so I didn't have to worry about being fashionable. I blended in and had the opportunity to reinvent myself. For the first time, I became interested in sports: football, basketball, and track. Track stuck all the way through college. I had the build for it—my brother's nickname for me at the time was "Ribcage."

Instead of being the shy new kid, I blossomed into the smart, athletic guy that got all the girls. Things had never clicked like that until I was in the right environment. Back then I went by my middle name, Eugene, and one of my teachers started calling me "Eugenius." I won all kinds of awards for science and scored off the charts in reading assessments. Whenever opportunities came up that had to do with speaking or influencing people, I would get picked for those things. If we had group presentations, I did the talking.

When eighth grade ended and high school started, I had to transfer schools again. It was like starting junior high all over again, but on a bigger scale—my seventh-grade school was my new high school's feeder. But this time, I was prepared. Now I knew how to maneuver.

The biggest dilemma was still my clothes. I knew I was going back to school with those same fashion-conscious people. I refused to be in that situation again, regardless of what my parents' financial situation looked like. I had two options. One: Hope that one of my parents would figure something out overnight and magically buy me a bunch of fancy name-brand clothes. Or two: Take matters into my own hands.

Around that time my friend Joby was working weekends for a reverend's ministry, selling pamphlets. Reverend Brown had kids in front of grocery stores hocking religious pamphlets for $2, of which he kept $1.25. It didn't take Joby long to start selling his for $5.

By this point, I knew how to talk to people. I have a nice voice. I'm charismatic. I was introduced to the reverend, loaded up my backpack with those pamphlets, and went out selling them on Friday evenings and all day on Saturdays. The reverend would come around in his van and drop as many as ten of us off in front of grocery stores in the nice parts of Dallas and Fort Worth. He tried to put us out there in pairs, but the other guys didn't have the work ethic that I did. Sometimes they wouldn't show up because they wanted to play basketball or something. I was out there every weekend. I wanted to *work*. At the end of the day, I'd end up with $100 or $200 in cash, come home, and stuff it all in a shoebox. Soon I had more clothes and shoes than I'd ever had in my life.

"Reverend" Brown ultimately proved to be a highly unscrupulous individual. No one had been to his church, and I don't think one ever existed. We were essentially panhandling for him, saying one program was for battered women, another for fatherless children, another for the homeless. We never saw any of that materialize. It was a money grab for him. I didn't fully realize until I got older: *man, he was pimping us!*

Meanwhile, back at school, I won't say that I had my *choice* of the ladies, but the girls I was interested in were responding. My mom was working as a teacher's aide during the day and at Subway at night. I was at home every day for several hours by myself. In those years I got into a lot of things I probably shouldn't have.

By my sophomore year, my eighth-grade girlfriend transferred to my high school, and we got back together. It wasn't quite love—I'll call it teenage infatuation. She got pregnant, and I became a father my junior year. It was never a good relationship. For the next several years, we were on and off at best. All the while, it went from bad to worse. At first I didn't tell my parents anything about the pregnancy. Then she started showing. Her mom called my mom, and then my mom called me.

"You and your girlfriend got something to tell me?"

I was like, *Nope!*

"Well, I talked to her mom, and apparently she's pregnant."

I felt like my world was falling apart. The fear of the unknown was overwhelming. I still thank my mom for being as supportive as she was. Her attitude was, "Hey, we'll get through this. It'll be fine. You don't need to drop out of school." But I was immediately thinking, *I gotta make more money*. The pamphlet money in my shoebox went from buying Jordans and jeans to diapers and milk.

The pamphlet money in my shoebox went from buying Jordans and jeans to diapers and milk.

From day one, my biggest thing was just *being there*, and I was there every day. I changed diapers, burped the little guy, fed him, and bought him clothes. Where I'm from, a lot of people don't even know who the heck their dad *is*. Even at seventeen, I refused to be that guy. It played a significant part in how my life went and who I am now. My childhood ended, and I had to grow up fast. I'm still trying to figure out hobbies, because they all went out the window as soon as I became a father. It's never been the same.

I had to ditch the pamphlet hustle and get a real job. I was recruited at the mall to work at a survey marketing company. I would stand around and ask the pretty girls walking by to do taste tests, and they got five dollars out of it. At the same time, the Subway my mom was working for was owned by a family friend, so I went to work there with my mom, my brother, *and* my sister.

The owner, Miss Valerie Session, was very frugal, serious about business, and dedicated to her customers. And at the time, my brother and I were just teenage slackers. We would pack up our PlayStation, hook it up to the TV in the back, and be back there playing Madden.

She called us in one day and told us to not bring it back. "You're here to work."

"Yes, Miss Session."

We were contrite for about ten minutes. We went to clean the soda machine, made some sandwiches, then turned the PlayStation right back on. Almost immediately, she snuck back up on us. My little skinny, scared self was all nervous she would fire us, but she gave us another chance.

Slowly, we started to observe how she ran that Subway. The same customers would come in every single day. She knew all their names, their orders, where they worked. The line could be outside the door during the lunch rush, but she was always cool, calm, and collected, greeting everybody with a smile. She owned the entire store but was still out there cutting sandwiches. A lot of people in her shoes would have been completely hands off. That taught me a lot. We learned a lot about customer service and even culture—she was a Christian woman. She would have gospel music playing over the speakers, and when something went wrong, she would be quick to pray with you.

My brother and I would try to lock the door at 8:50 p.m. to close for the night at nine, and here she comes at 8:55 p.m., making sure we're on the ball. I can't believe she kept us around. We regularly burned cookies and bread. She was so kind and forgiving. But if you burned or messed something up, she would look at it, then she'd look at you, and then *you* bought it—you may as well take it home. If you burned a batch of cookies, it was coming out of your check. Subways are not cheap to run—the unit cost of their six-inch bread was fifty cents, and they were selling sandwiches for four bucks.

We had a lot of fun working together, cracking jokes, talking about what we were going to do in the future. We both knew that how we grew up was not how we wanted our futures to look. We were both into the ladies but didn't have any money making $5.15 an hour. But what does every girl like? Food! I would be bringing girls fresh Subway cookies and sandwiches *all* the time, and it worked. I would even bring dates there, because I definitely couldn't afford the movies. Always resourceful. The only thing I didn't like was smelling like a loaf of bread at the end of every day.

With my mom helping with the baby, my life was Subway, doing surveys at the mall, and track practice, I spent the entire summer before college trying to earn my way onto a track team. I was winning competition after competition, and all the track coaches started following my progress. I jumped 6'6" and easily won the local Fort Worth–area championship. Then I hit 6'8" at the regionals and ended up ranked third in the nation. Two or three weeks later, I was headed to the Junior Olympics at Purdue University and had to get on a charter bus to drive up there. That's when cell phones still charged for roaming out of state, and I didn't know. When I got back, my cell phone bill was over $300. My mom was still paying for it, and she threw a fit.

The top guy coming in had jumped 7'1", and another guy had jumped 6'10". I was so cocky and overconfident. I was coming in at 6'8", thinking, *I have a shot at this.* I had a little ritual before competitions where I would intimidate people. During warm-ups, the attendants would raise the bar up to let everyone get their approaches and measurements straight. Everyone was practicing at 5'8" or so. I would stroll up, ask the attendants to raise it all the way up to six feet, do a little jog over to the bar in my sweats, scissor right over it, then smile at the other guys like *Y'all have no chance.* Usually, it worked. I'd get in their heads, and they'd fall out. I wouldn't even start the competition until the bar got up to six feet. At that point, most of the others already dropped out before I even started.

But it did *not* go that way at the Junior Olympics. They opened the bar at 5'10". There are still photos of me online clearing it. After that, I couldn't even clear six feet. To this day I still don't know what happened. I was in tears. This continued all the way through college. Things just went downhill from the day I jumped 6'8". I never made it that high again.

I still had a track scholarship offer waiting at a junior college in Oklahoma. My high school coach had a relationship with theirs. My coach told me point-blank: "Take it. It's a done deal." I was like, "Nope. Can't leave my son." I proceeded to put all my eggs in one basket and applied to University of North Texas. I only found out that I'd been rejected two weeks after the letter was delivered. My mom had been holding on to it. When I finally found out, she told me, "I didn't want to tell you—I didn't want you to be disappointed."

But I've never been a quitter. I don't take bad news and just fold. There's always a way around. I don't take people's opinions as the final word on anything. My attitude was, *Let's see what we can do.* I went to their website, started researching, and found out that I could apply for what they called an "individual review." Through that, I ended up getting a meeting with the dean of enrollment. I went in and sat there for sixty minutes selling him on why I should be admitted. It worked. I met with the track coaches next, and they brought me onto the team.

My first year of college went well. I earned my highest grade point average of all time, adjusted to being a college athlete, and generally had a good time. For the first time in my life, I established a solid core of friends from the track team. My friend Tim was there for me when my financial aid fell through as a sophomore and I had nowhere to live. He was still living with his parents twenty minutes from campus, let me move in for two months, and never charged me a thing.

Rob was my other best friend—a six-foot-four Will Smith lookalike but with green eyes, and one of the coolest people I've ever met. I can blame Rob for some of my ambition. His dad was a retired professional football player, and one day we went back home with him to pick something up. When we got to his neighborhood in Plano, I had never seen houses like that in my life. It was like the neighborhoods I used to Rollerblade through, but on a whole new level. All over again I'm wondering, *What do these people do for a living? I gotta figure this thing out.* I couldn't shake the thought of having a nice house in a nice neighborhood like that. I just kept thinking, *I have to live like this one day.*

Soon thereafter, I had my second son. I was in nutrition class when my then-girlfriend, Ashlee, texted that she was going into labor. I dashed out of class, flew down the highway to the hospital, and was there with her for three days. From then on, baby Ashton was with me in my dorm every weekend. It was always me, Rob, Tim, and the kids. Three men and two babies. I'd often be in my dorm room with both my sons, watching them play on the floor. Sometimes I couldn't help thinking, *Man, y'all don't look nothing alike. I know y'all have different moms, but Ashton looks a* lot *like me.*

I always just let it go.

You're not defined by your circumstances, whether good or bad—you're defined by the lessons you learn and how you implement them to improve your life. There are two sides to every coin, and two sides to every event: positive and negative. Whichever you focus on will eventually shape your character.

My becoming a father at sixteen could have been an adverse event, but it taught me the value of hard work—especially when someone else depends on you. As a father of four, that particular lesson still drives me today.

Get a piece of paper and write down the three adverse events that were significant to you. Take a few minutes to reflect on them, and find a positive lesson in each. Make the positive insights you gain from this exercise the story you tell yourself from now on. Being a victim isn't your fault, but suffering is. When you dwell on negative events and stories, you'll rob yourself of the momentum you need to accomplish great things.

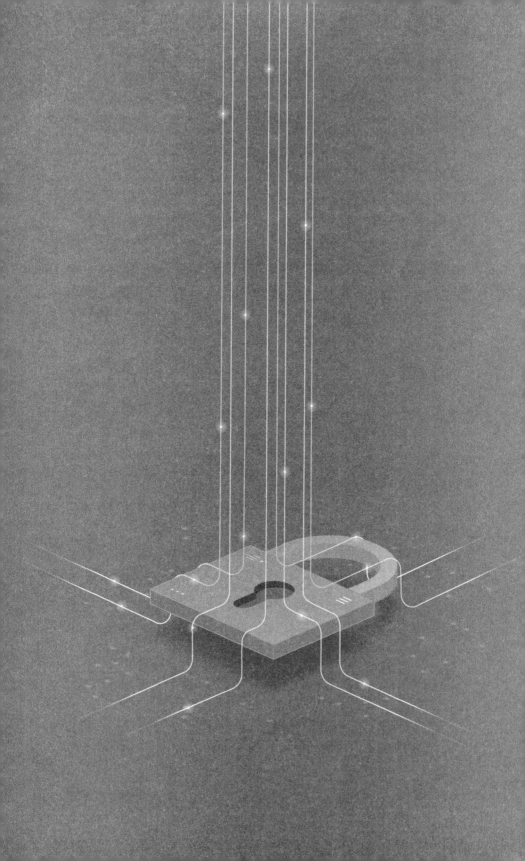

CHAPTER 2

Trouble

By this point, I had already had seven or eight cars—all raggedy, piece-of-junk buckets. In college, I was driving a red 1986 Honda Prelude. It was rusty and broke down a few times, but otherwise ran decent. After spending $600 to buy it, I couldn't afford the parking pass for campus. I was constantly sneaking my car to different locations at night. They eventually caught up to me and impounded it. They wanted payment for over $1,000 in tickets, so I just let them keep it.

I eventually replaced it with a 1992 Mazda MX-6, and eventually finally found enough money to afford that $400 campus parking pass. When I went to their office to get it, they immediately pulled up all my unpaid tickets. Meanwhile, I saw some of their people outside, running the license plate on the car I drove up in. I shot out of the building, jumped into the car, threw it in reverse, and *bam*, collided with the University of North Texas ticketing car.

I panicked, sped out of the parking lot, and suddenly found myself on a high-speed chase. I was driving entirely too fast through campus, probably doing fifty, flying by the twenty-mile-per-hour speed limit signs. Of course I was concerned I was going to hit somebody, but the fight-or-flight instinct just took over. I made it off campus and ran a light at the corner. By the time I hit the freeway, I didn't see anyone in my rearview. It felt like something out of an action movie.

The car chase was Friday. When I showed up to track practice on Monday, my coach was like, "LeBoyd, what kind of trouble did you get into this weekend?"

"What are you talking about? Me? Trouble?"

He handed me a card and said a detective was looking for me. When I went to buy that parking pass, I had been wearing my track uniform. The cops went straight to the team's website, looked at the roster, found me, and issued a warrant for my arrest: leaving the scene of an accident.

I told my dad. He drove me to the police station, where I was handcuffed and walked into jail. I had no idea about bail processes, bondsmen, or anything like that. Knowing what I know now, I would've handled everything differently—I never would've even set foot inside the place.

You think you're prepared for jail by having seen so much of it on TV. But I didn't *really* know what to expect. I thought people were gonna be messing with me and that I was going to have to be watching my manhood. But at that time, my hair was pretty long, and I'd taken my braids down. I looked like a crazy person. My mug shot's still out there on the internet, and I look like Sideshow Bob.

There were several people around, but nothing crazy happened. What I then learned was that whenever you go to jail, everybody's innocent. Nobody did a thing. The whole time, everyone just talked about how innocent they were. I was in for seven or eight hours. They brought food, which I refused to eat. Most of all, it was so cold in there. I remember having my arms inside my shirt, freezing.

The cops eventually told me I could pay $800 for a pretrial diversion, and if I stayed out of trouble for six months, my infraction would disappear from my record. I didn't have $800, and my parents didn't have $800. Guess what? I had to go on deferred adjudication, which is a conviction. Now I had a misdemeanor on my record, and I would be on probation for the next two years.

That wasn't my last car chase either. The guy that I bought the Mazda from, Juan Jesús, was essentially running a car dealership out of his house, setting up shady payment plans with people. I don't know what I was thinking trying to finance a car through this crazy guy with no money. I'd had the Mazda a little over a year when one night, at Ashlee's house, Juan snuck over to clandestinely repossess it. I wasn't late on payments, and to this day I still don't know what he was thinking.

As soon as we noticed the car was gone, we went on a late-night covert operation to steal it back. We got in Ashlee's car and crept through one apartment complex parking lot after another. After an hour or so, we finally found it. It was a strange feeling, tiptoeing over and breaking into my own car. I was so nervous my leg was shaking. I started it up, and just as I was about to drive off, Juan Jesús came running out of his apartment, like he'd been waiting for me to show up. He jumped into *his* car and started chasing me.

Now, normally, my car was fast. But now I was shifting like crazy, and something was off. It didn't matter how much gas I gave it; it wouldn't go above thirty. I started panicking even more, wondering what he did to the car. Did he take out a spark plug? Did he put sugar in the tank? The thing would just not *go*.

Meanwhile, Juan Jesús was in his BMW M3, and he starts ramming me. Psychotic. I was freaking out so much that I called the police. "Hey! This guy's ramming me! He's tearing me up!" I'm frantic and yelling on the phone, and they did not care. He eventually hit my car from the side, like the police do in car chases to make whoever's fleeing spin out.

Now I was stuck in this otherwise tranquil residential area, seeing red and ready to fight. I'm trying to get out of the car to light the guy up, but the door is jammed, and I was basically trapped inside. Meanwhile, he must have seen how furious I was, thought the better of it, and just drove off.

I went straight back to Ashlee's mom's house, walked in, and called the people that buy junk cars, no questions asked. They gave me three hundred bucks, took it away, and I've never seen it since.

By this time, my life was class, track, and pushing carts at a grocery store called Sack and Save. I *hated* that place. I took to calling it "Sack and Slave." They were paying me something like five dollars and change per hour. It wasn't a lot, but it helped pay for diapers. By the time I got there, I was inevitably tired and burned out. I would hide in the room where they painted the sale signs and sleep until I heard my name on the intercom. "LeBoyd! We need cart service!" It didn't matter what the weather was like, you had to go get those carts.

But I didn't ultimately stick around for very long. One day my mom called, and when I picked it up, my manager got right on my case.

"You can't be on the phone out here."

I was already tired, and I went off. "You're going to tell me when I can and cannot answer my own phone? If my mom calls, I'm gonna answer. I'll answer my phone whenever I *want to!*" I also informed her I didn't need the stupid job anyway.

She says, "Well, give me your badge. You can go *right now*."

I still remember going back to my dorm room after it all went down. When I walked in, Rob looked up at me. "The hell you doing here?"

"I quit."

In the meantime, I'd taken up a little side hustle. A buddy of mine was selling weed and had it around in large quantities. When I saw how he was living, I asked how I could get in. When he told me the buy-in cost, of course I didn't have the money. I'm not proud of this, but I stole another student's laptop and pawned it to get the cash. It was so dumb. I was nineteen. I wasn't thinking about tracking systems.

In any case, I never got caught, and we used to chop and bag the product right there in my dorm room. My college was in a predominantly white area. I knew the police were profiling, and I didn't want to give them any reason to be suspicious. Driving around making deliveries, I would wear crisp, clean Polo button-ups on top where they were visible, and basketball shorts and Jordans beneath and out of sight.

That didn't always work. One day I got pulled over, and they gave me a ticket for not having insurance. A few months later, I got pulled over again. The car had heavily tinted windows, and I was smoking a cigar with the window cracked. The cop pulled me over for allegedly having a taillight out. I didn't buy it. My sister had just had the car completely fixed and cleaned up. I got out to look. "Dude, how is the taillight out? This car just got out of the shop."

It didn't matter. He ran my ID and said, "Well, buddy, your license is suspended, and you're driving, so you're going to jail."

At the time, I had a flip phone, and I quickly got it out to call my dad. "I just got pulled over, and my license is suspended, so they're gonna take me to jail."

Of course, the officer is immediately telling me to get off the phone. Here we go again: someone telling me when I can or cannot use the phone.

"Nah, man. I'm *not* getting off the phone."

I'm talking a little faster to my dad now. "They're getting ready to take me to jail. Get a lawyer, do something, do whatever you can. I need you to get me out!" Again, the officer's commanding me to get off the phone.

"Man, I'm talking to my dad. Can't you see who I'm talking to?"

At this, the cop took my phone and snapped it in half with his bare hands. Then he picked *me* up, slammed me on the trunk, and handcuffed me. I'm screaming, "What are you doing, dude? This is completely unnecessary! I'm just trying to get my dad to come bail me out of jail!"

He threw me in the back of the squad car—a very unpleasant experience.

When I got to jail, it was the same thing all over again. Freezing cold; everyone's innocent. When I got out and they gave me my possessions back in the standard clear plastic bag, there was my flip phone, snapped in half, somehow still ringing. You could still answer and talk into it, but you couldn't hear what the other person was saying.

Both times I was pulled over, I was thinking: What if I'd also had weed on me? It gradually dawned on me: *if you want to be the guy you've always said you were going to be, you can't be taking these kinds of risks.* I'm telling this story here because my students tell me all the time: "I've been arrested, so I can't get a job." I'm not trying to hear that. I am *not* trying to hear it.

Around the same time, Ashlee got pregnant again, and we were shocked when she went into traumatic labor five months premature. Even the doctors didn't believe her until she started going into labor right there in the ER waiting room. When they brought her in, they discovered that the baby was having an aneurysm. The doctor ultimately told us that if the baby made it, she'd be in a lifelong vegetative state. We had to make the decision to take Paige off the ventilator, wrapped her in a little blanket, and passed her around to say our goodbyes.

Sometimes tragedy hits, and you respond by relentlessly focusing on next steps. This was a live birth, so she had to be buried. I was too broke to pay for a funeral. The state will pay for funerals, but it's gonna be on their schedule, so we had to wait three days. In the meantime, we went to find a dress to bury her in. She was so small. She fit in the palm of my hand, and there's no way you can find a dress for someone that small. We had to go to the store and buy a Barbie dress because it's the only thing that would fit her.

My life went downhill. I gave up, stopped working, stopped going to class. All I could do was focus on what I had lost. With no money to pay rent, I got evicted. I moved back in with Mom, where we lived like roommates. For a time, I had no hope for the future. My dreams of being successful went out the window.

Not that there were a lot of successful people around. I would see people in my neighborhood outside on the street, drinking. I called them *bird watchers. Y'all are out here with nothing to do. Just fricking watching birds.* On one hand, it got on my nerves: *get a job!* On the other, I felt like I was heading down that path myself.

I tried to focus on my kids and making my daughter proud— Paige wouldn't want me hanging around being miserable, not being a productive citizen. I really had to lean on my faith, because I didn't have the power to recover on my own. I was just praying to God for the strength and wisdom to do *something* and shake me out of that rut, because I didn't feel like doing *anything*.

> I was just praying to God for the strength and wisdom to do *something* and shake me out of that rut, because I didn't feel like doing *anything*.

Meanwhile, I was on academic probation, so I couldn't go back to University of North Texas. When you don't complete classes and get all those zeros, your GPA goes down the tank. I enrolled at a junior college nearby. I was able to use a school loan to pay for the classes, and it also gave me some money to cover living expenses. For a month I was in class, trying to get things back together and come out of the dark.

But I still wasn't making any money. Ever heard of Rainbow vacuum cleaners? That's the first thing I tried. I saw an ad in the classifieds that claimed you could make twenty-five dollars an hour selling them. Well, yes, sir! That was a lot of money for me. It was a commission-only job. I was going into people's homes, vacuuming, showing them how dirty their carpets were, and how good this $3,000 vacuum was at sucking everything up. I was committed to it. And I made zero dollars.

I tried to go work for Walmart to get a job in produce. When they saw that first car chase on my record, even *they* turned me down. Then, miraculously, my friend Rob introduced me to his friend D. J., whose uncle was making a bunch of money at AT&T doing phone sales.

D. J. introduced me to his uncle, and he set me up with an interview, which I killed. It was like the clouds parted. Even though I was just going to be a guy selling cell phones in a call center, it meant so much more. Number one, it was in Plano, where I had first started to really imagine a future for myself. Just the energy of being there made me feel like things were about to start taking shape. Number two, I was in a call center and working with warm inbound leads, so I didn't have to go door-to-door. Third, it was the highest-paying job I had ever had in my life. It was immediately clear: this was gonna be it for me. I accepted the job, signed on the dotted line, and started training the following Monday.

No one escapes experiencing traumatic events. They're part of life. Many people never recover from a personal tragedy. I was almost one of them.

Most people don't recover because they don't have anything to look forward to. We want to make sure that doesn't happen to you. When your why is strong enough, you can overcome anything.

So define your why. Get a sheet of paper, sit in a quiet place, and close your eyes for five minutes. It's time to dream. Think about what excites you and what you want to accomplish in life. Maybe it's buying a dream house or car. The only thing that matters is that it means something to you. Write down what you want out of life. Form a vivid picture in your mind. Your why can be an item or a statement. My why was to never see my children struggle like I did when I was a kid.

When you're done, place that sheet of paper in your purse or wallet and keep it close, because you'll need it when times get tough.

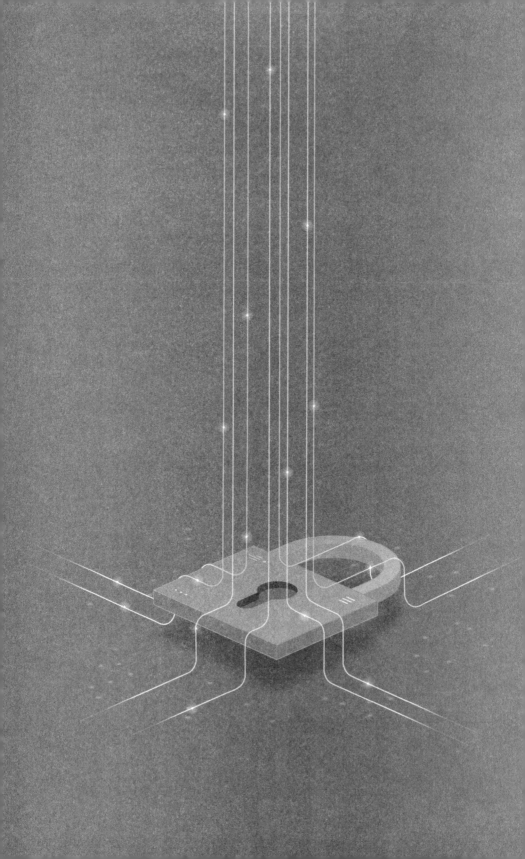

CHAPTER 3

IT

—

On day one of training, I got a call from Denton County. See you in court. Tomorrow.

I had to deal with that charge for driving with a suspended license, and AT&T had a strict training policy. After getting hired, you needed to complete the entire first week of training, and you were not allowed to miss a single day, hour, or minute—period.

I went and talked to the guy that hired me. "Look. I just have to be honest with you. I got into some trouble a few months ago, and I have to go to court tomorrow. If I don't, I'm going to jail. Is there any way I can join the next training class?"

He heard me out and went to see what he could do. "I've talked to HR. Everything's fine. You can start in three weeks."

I wound up with a court-appointed attorney, but a good one. Somehow, he got my arrest downgraded into a ticket for "failing to identify myself." I still don't know how that makes sense or how he worked that magic. It helped that the judge could see that I was legitimately not a bad kid. For that I'm eternally grateful to Judge Virgil

Vahlencamp. He accepted the invented charge and didn't revoke my probation. These situations should not have worked out the way that they did. I can only thank God, because it could have been worse—a *lot* worse. But it still took years to pay all those court fees. Years!

When I ultimately went into training, everything just made sense to me. I'm a natural salesperson. I came out and just immediately started doing well. I'd been at these jobs that were paying seven dollars per hour. Now I was making twelve dollars an hour, plus commissions. That was big money for me.

One of the ways they kept us motivated was to remind us of *why* we were trying to make sales in the first place. We had to get literal with our goals. Mine was a convertible. I printed off a picture of a Chrysler Sebring, one of the cheapest convertibles out there, and tacked it up in my cubicle.

Soon I had the money to buy not one, but two. Clew-1 and Clew-2. One was burgundy, and the other one was fire red with a peanut butter interior. Yes, indeed. I drove everywhere with the top down. It didn't matter what the weather was doing. I'm always cold by nature, but I *still* had the top down, driving down the road, freezing.

I also made enough money to get my own apartment. Ashlee and I still couldn't afford to live in Plano, so we moved to Lewisville. After work I'd still cruise through Plano, looking at all the nice houses. *One day, man, this is going to be me.* I started to realize more concretely that *seeing* things that I aspired to helped. It pushed me. I'm purpose driven. If I'm not working toward a specific goal, I'm not going to be successful.

I ended up becoming one of the top salespeople at AT&T very quickly. Instead of trying to sell people individual things, I would build a creative package deal and give people one price. They were always responding, "Oh, I get all that, *included?*" I started calling it the Clewis Bundle. Eight months in, I was crushing it. I was twenty years old and making over $4,000 a month with only a high school diploma.

When Memorial Day rolled around, they didn't have enough staff on hand to support all the incoming calls. I volunteered to come in and ended up selling twenty-three phones in eight hours, which was some kind of record.

The higher-ups noticed. They started reviewing my calls to pick up on what I was doing. One of my managers decided that my Clewis Bundle was against their code of business conduct. They called it *slamming*. That manager was an older black guy, which made the whole episode even worse. I thought our people looked out for one another! In the meeting where they fired me, he was hostile toward me, almost to the point where he was yelling at me across the table.

The case went to arbitration, and the Communication Workers Union got involved. I wasn't hiding anything. I always broke everything down for my customers. Whether or not it was fair, I was now in another horrible situation, with an apartment and a car I couldn't afford. It's not like I had savings. I'd been burning every dollar, and my accounts were overdrawn every week. I was really banking on the whole arbitration thing getting settled, thinking I was going to get all this back pay. I thought it was going to be easy to overturn, but I never got the job back.

It was a struggle to find something new. I went to work for Verizon, except it wasn't *really* Verizon. I found a listing in the green sheets from a company called Encore Marketing, who claimed one could make twenty-five dollars per hour selling cellular services. I went in, filled out an application, and did an interview, and they gave me the job on the spot. I didn't know exactly what this was all going to entail, but I didn't care—I just needed a job.

They told me that Verizon outsourced a deal to them, and that they generally needed B2B salespeople. Basically, if a business didn't have Verizon as their telephone carrier, we tried to get them to switch. And if they were already using Verizon, then we had to try to get them on a better plan.

It was supposed to pay a ton of money, but again, it was 100 percent commission based. You picked a territory, went door-to-door, and tried to talk to business owners. I ended up getting a few deals my first month and made around $3,000. Not bad, but not nearly what I was making at AT&T. The next month didn't go as well. I made a few sales but didn't make their quota. As a result, they didn't pay me *at all*. I flipped out and called my manager, screaming and cussing. I'd been out there working, still made sales, and they just robbed me. I quit.

Next, I got a gig working for a company called Real Page as a "virtual leasing agent." When people would call in for information about an apartment complex they saw online, they got routed to me. I was making eight bucks an hour setting up apartment tours. That eight dollars an hour wasn't cutting it. The job was so low paying and boring that I only lasted two months.

I got evicted from my apartment in Lewisville and went back to live with my mom—again. Then we found out that Ashlee was pregnant—again. We got married and managed to move into a little apartment. I just wanted my children to grow up in the same house and to be the best father I could. After we got married, the main thing I remember is not having any money for a honeymoon. We didn't even get a hotel room. My mom just kept the kids for the weekend.

Meanwhile, the second I had started making bank back at AT&T, my high school girlfriend had put me on child support. In Texas, they don't care whether you have a job or not. After taking care of the little guy for four years, she told the state that I'd never provided any support, ever. Suddenly I had to pay her $210 a month, which was significant for me at the time. Next, they hit me with four years' worth of arrears, and I got this huge bill in the mail.

After years of this toxic relationship and noticing how different my two sons looked, I finally decided to do a DNA test. They shipped it to my dorm room, and I swabbed the both of us. Turns out he *wasn't* my son.

Right away, I called my mom. "What's the name of that divorce attorney you used?" He informed me that if you sign an acknowledgment of paternity in the state of Texas, you're *legally* a father whether you're *actually* the father or not. I had signed at sixteen, so I got out of it on account of having been a minor.

When it was all finalized, his mother didn't even show up to court. I haven't seen either of them since. Of course, I had conflicting emotions, but mostly I was relieved that I could leave a toxic relationship behind and that my new wife wouldn't have to be a stepmom.

All the while I was dealing with different staffing companies, dressing up in a suit and tie, just trying like crazy to get a job. I'd gotten a taste of making good money, and all these other jobs were paying peanuts. It haunted me for years. I just could not seem to get back to the amount of money I was making at AT&T.

I finally ended up landing a job at Ricoh, one of the largest copier companies in the world. I started in the accounting department, working on contracts. My immediate problem there was learning things *too* quickly. On my first day, the supervisor that hired me showed me how to validate contracts. She gave me a huge stack to process and told me we'd review them the next day. "It'll probably take you through the end of the day to get it all done."

I was like, *Okay, cool.* Then I knocked out the whole stack in two hours. When I finished, my supervisor was nowhere to be found. At that point, I did what any young guy with time on his hands would do: I started watching a movie on my computer. At some point she returned and saw me sitting there but didn't say anything. Then, instead of addressing me directly, she called the staffing agency that placed me. "This LeBoyd guy is playing on the computer when he's supposed to be working!"

The staffing agency then hung up with her and called *me*. Meanwhile, my supervisor's three cubicles over. I'm like, "Hey! I finished the work that she asked me to do, and she disappeared. It's my first day. I don't know what else to do. She could have just asked me what was going on!"

We got it figured out, and the job ended up being good. It definitely helped financially. My wife wasn't working outside the house, so that burden was all on me. I was only making thirteen dollars per hour, but that was the highest per-hour rate I'd ever made. More importantly, I learned they had offered something that I'd never heard of: unlimited overtime. There was so much work that needed to be done. They were so behind on auditing those contracts that I started working sixty hours a week, getting time and a half for a third of it. This went on for over two years.

I tried to move up onto their sales team, but that required a bachelor's degree. I was putting in applications elsewhere, but I wasn't getting any callbacks. Looking back, my résumé was weak, and I didn't do a good job of branding the skills that I had.

But I *did* start to learn more about technology. We used an Oracle database system to review these contracts, and I had never worked with that type of technology before. I was only just starting to understand how to navigate computers. Before then, I really didn't know anything about them.

Ricoh is based out of Japan, and their support staff worked at their American headquarters in New Jersey. Whenever a desktop or a laptop would break, the employees at the Dallas office would have to ship it all the way up to New Jersey to be repaired, then wait for it to be shipped back. Meanwhile, that computerless employee was just sitting idle. When that happened, their work got dumped on the people that were good at it, such as yours truly. I started thinking, *I'm gonna fix this for you, because I'm tired of doing your work.*

I eventually started setting up user accounts for new hires and fixing minor software issues at the office. It started off on a volunteer basis for a few hours a week, but gradually I became the unofficial office IT guy. I didn't have the confidence to get out and start applying for IT jobs, but I knew it was something I could do if I set my mind to it. Nearly all the fixes were simple. A light bulb went off in my mind: *you're in the wrong field, buddy.*

Sometimes the universe has a way of speeding up your plans. One day in April, the Ricoh leadership flew in from Japan to visit the Dallas office. We were all so excited. "The CEO's coming! Let's make everything look presentable!"

The C-suite rolled up and told us the company's goals and vision. Then they told us they were closing operations in Dallas, and that we would all be let go.

If you stayed on for your last sixty days, you got a severance package: one week's salary for every year that you worked for the company. I'd been there two and a half years total, but only one as a full-time employee, so I was screwed there. At least they filed for unemployment on our collective behalf. That amounted to about $400 a week.

Believe it or not, this was *exciting* to me. I immediately went and did something radical. Unlike AT&T, Ricoh gave us the *insight* that we were going to be let go ahead of time. Now I had the opportunity to prepare.

First off, the apartment that I was living in with my wife at the time was expensive—the nicest I'd ever had. We knew that we were going to have to move. We downgraded and went back to the hood, where our rent was $299 a month.

Meanwhile, one of my coworkers at Ricoh told me she had a computer she didn't use. That piqued my curiosity.

"What kind of computer are we talking about here?"

"I think it's called an iMac? It's pretty much brand new. I still have the box."

It was a twenty-one-inch iMac. I had never had anything that fancy in my life. She sold it to me for four hundred bucks, and it was worth four times that. That was my first actual computer. I didn't have one during college, because I couldn't afford it.

Ricoh brought in consultants for a three-day workshop to help us revamp our résumés and counsel us on how to move forward. When I told one of the consultants about my ambitions, she said her son was making seventy dollars an hour in IT. I was clearly headed in the right direction.

By that point, I understood something that most people just refuse to admit. You know what that is? Racism! Believe it or not, it exists! When we were revamping our résumés, I kept looking at my name on paper. I kept seeing the "Le" at the beginning of my name. It just screamed out *black guy*. This may sound bad: I stopped and thought, *If I'm thinking this about my own résumé, what are hiring managers thinking when they look at it?*

I decided that I was going to reinvent myself. I wanted to give myself every opportunity imaginable. No limits. My thought process has always been, "If I can get the interview, I can get the job." I resolved to just play the game. I'll pimp the system and try something new.

> I decided that I was going to reinvent myself. I wanted to give myself every opportunity imaginable. No limits.

What happens if I drop the Le from my name and become Boyd? I updated my résumé, updated my LinkedIn profile, created a new email address, and Boyd is who I became from that day forward. I'm not the Boyd that people used to know. Today, I even have a little joke when girls tell people they used to date me: *Nah, you dated LeBoyd. You did not date Boyd. We are not the same.*

Another first: Instead of talking about my accounts receivable experience, I only talked about doing tech support. In other words, for the first time, I started to present myself as an IT professional. I still teach my students: when it comes to your job experience and your résumé, it's *your* story. You can tell that story however you want, as long as it's factual. I wanted to be an IT professional, and African Americans are underrepresented in tech. Some people might look at what I did and say it was dishonest. I'd just say that I was being targeted.

I went to Walmart and bought myself a $300 laptop to tinker with. Ashlee got mad that I bought this little Acer for the price of our monthly rent, and we got in a fight about it. We still had no money, I was still unemployed, and she saw that I already had a perfectly good computer. But there's only so much you can do at a desktop. You can't take that thing anywhere! She didn't talk to me for two or three days. Of course, the entire point of buying the computer was to figure this stuff out and get a job, but she did not see my vision.

It blew over, and meanwhile, we were settling into a new church. With my dad being a preacher growing up, I was always in church. Especially throughout high school, I was at church every Sunday. When I went off to college, I didn't attend as much because it was just a bunch of old people showing up—everyone my age was away at school. When I got deeply involved again, it really aided my career. I showed up like, *Hey, I don't have a job, but I have time.* I became part of their production team and am the director of technology there to this day. I learned more about computers, cameras, lighting, and everything else needed to produce the service. I'd never dealt with technology like that before.

As we progressed, stuff started happening. There was the guy there by the name of Elvis Bowman, and he's one of the smartest people I've ever met. The guy can sing, play the piano, write web applications, edit videos, and take photos. There's nothing that guy can't do. He's not only a genius but also willing to teach anyone that was willing to learn.

He needed help updating the church's website and uploading videos. Today it's easy, but back then there was more to it. Among other things, you had to edit code, and I had no idea how to do that.

After church on Sundays, Elvis would show me things, then give me the responsibility of taking care of them. I learned how to read web configurations, edit HTML, and do all kinds of other skills that would pay off in the future, all in service unto the Lord. I wouldn't have gotten my start in IT without that experience at the church, and I have Elvis to thank for it.

Before too long, one of my laid-off coworkers told me about a company out of Chicago called Creative Ventures. They were offering free online IT training for people that had been laid off. Immediately, I was like, *Gimme, gimme, gimme. Where do I sign?* In no time, I started and finished Introduction to Computers. It was my first IT certification. They even gave me a certificate once I finished.

Once I had that, I was studying like a madman, submitting job applications from sunup to sundown. I was hell-bent on getting into IT. I took another certification exam and passed it on my first attempt. The minute they gave me a certification number for that, I put it on LinkedIn. I was submitting application after application, but for a long time, nobody was calling back.

I finally landed an interview with a small company called Tekcenture, which was owned by Indian immigrants. I felt knowledgeable enough, and the interview went well. And at the end of the interview, I asked an all-important question, and one I teach to my students now: Is there any reason that you wouldn't give me this job based on everything we've discussed? It gives you a chance to address objections. Many people feel like they killed their job interviews, then are surprised when they never get a call back.

They said, "You don't have the experience we're looking for. But we really like you. We're going to hire you, *and* we're going to teach you. We'll start you off with a salary of $36,000 for ninety days. If it works out, we'll bump your salary up to $40K." I was speechless. This was the highest-paying job I've ever had, and it didn't require me to sell anything. All I had to do was tech support, *and* they were going to teach me. I was getting paid $40,000 to learn!

Tekcenture provided IT outsourcing for several small businesses: accounting firms, marketing companies, car dealerships, etcetera. My position was to provide support across all these different verticals. I was learning so much. I finally had a stable career. I had never experienced so much joy working in my life. I was having fun *every day*.

When they ultimately raised my salary to $40K, I went and bought myself a Mustang. The standard for how computers operate and communicate with each other is called TCP/IP. After I bought the Mustang, I had a custom TCP/IP license plate made. People would see it and be like, "Dude, you must really love what you do." Yes. Absolutely. I was in heaven. We got out of that little apartment in the hood and rented a big old house in Arlington.

Soon, another one of my old friends from Ricoh reached out to me. Her friend owned an IT company, and they were looking for someone to do what I was already doing, but for a salary of $55,000. I went and told my boss that I was extremely grateful for everything they'd taught me, but that I was moving to another company to develop my career. He asked if there was anything they could do to get me to stay, but there was no way they were going to pay me sixty grand. The new company was called Cartish Technologies, and I was there doing tech support for a year.

Then I went and did something profoundly stupid. I started thinking that I could do it all myself. *Why do I need a middleman? My clients love me. I could run this business.* When I looked at my company's financials, they were making millions just doing simple tech support. Then I had one client come to me and say, "Hey, if you were to start your own company, I would go with you." So I started a business on the side doing computer repair and remote support and called it Aweteks. It still exists today, in a sense. I'd been telling myself for years, *Eventually you're going to make money*. Maybe this was it. I took that one client and put in my notice.

They gave me a decent retainer check, which I used to pay for an office, then had a big grand opening. So arrogant! So immature! I sat in the office for the next two months without a single new client. I had no idea how to market. I knew how to sell, but no idea how to attract customers. It got bad, and I started to panic. I was cold-calling businesses and getting hung up on. I couldn't even get the right people on the phone.

I got so desperate that I resorted to gimmicky marketing. I went to the scrub store, bought a doctor's jacket, got "Dr. Aweteks" embroidered on it, then went door-to-door trying to make sales as "the Computer Doctor." That did not work at all. I simply did not understand business. I had no foundation. You need to look at the big picture: sales, marketing, taxes, delivery. There's so much to be done, and I never considered any of it. I should have never quit that job.

But then, a miracle happened. Out of nowhere, I got a call from a recruiter. He said he was trying to fill a position at a software company called Tyler Technologies. "I'm having a lot of trouble—it's because of the shift. It pays thirty dollars an hour, but we need somebody that can work from 5:00 p.m. to 2:00 a.m."

I was like, "Perfect!"

He couldn't believe it. "Wait. Wait, are you serious?"

I'm thinking, *Hey, I'm up all night anyway. I can still run my own business during the day.*

"Of course. When can I start?"

You are the creator of your destiny. It's never too late to reinvent yourself or change careers. I changed my name, my career, and ultimately my life because of an intentional decision. I'm thankful for the Ricoh layoff. Without it, I probably wouldn't have made the transition into IT, because I was comfortable. I want you to think about what your comfort is costing you. Get a piece of paper, and answer these three questions:

Do you love your career so much that you'd work for free if you didn't need the money?

Are you excited about your career advancement opportunities?

Have you put your true passion on the back burner so that you can focus on collecting a paycheck at work?

Your answers to these questions will reveal how you truly feel about your career. If you aren't happy with your current job, give yourself permission to be happy anyway, then make the necessary adjustments to start the career of your dreams—even if it means jumping into a completely new industry or changing your name.

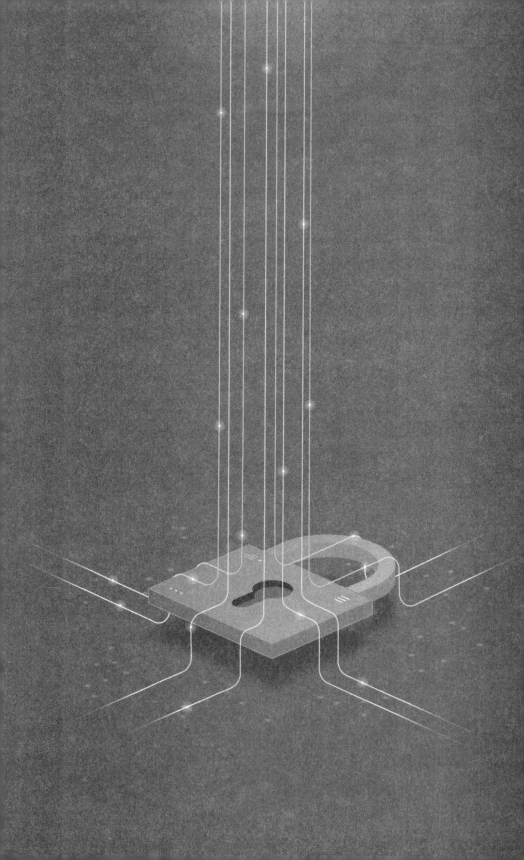

CHAPTER 4

Security

Meanwhile, Ashlee was still at home, taking care of the kids. Together, we were terrible at budgeting and managing money. When it was time to pay the bills, there was never any money left. With my salary, this should not have been the case. One morning after my midnight shift, I came out into the parking lot. Guess what was *not* there? My car. They repossessed it right there at the office. I have to point the finger. Ashlee had been buying clothes and shoes, giving money to her mom whenever she asked.

All the while I was thinking, *I need to make more money*. I studied IT more intensely and got more certifications, hoping I could get a better salary. The unique and unexpected opportunity at Tyler Technologies was working in a forty-thousand-square-foot building in the middle of the night by myself. As the only person there, I didn't have anyone asking for my time. As long as the system stayed up, I could do whatever I wanted. A group of really smart people had set up a very solid system there, so there were very few issues to deal with.

The weird hours were a blessing in disguise. I spent 10 percent of my time actually working, and I was ultimately there almost three years. Mostly I was just poking around, learning new stuff, accumulating knowledge. I looked into where the industry was headed and took a big interest in information security. The earning potential was huge.

Around that time, the Heartbleed vulnerability took the IT world by storm. Say you were on Nike.com, buying shoes. When Heartbleed came along, somebody could have stolen all your information from that page, including your credit card information—*as you were typing it*. Nothing was encrypted. When I tell you that the company and industry on a whole panicked ... they *panicked*. The impact it had on our organization, like most IT and security organizations, was huge.

Vulnerabilities were a new world to me. I became very interested in helping our organization become more secure. Cloud applications were just starting to come online, and it was clear that security was going to have to be at the forefront of every company's game plan. I just kept studying, studying, studying. After the layoff, I had already formed a study addiction. Every day I spent hours on YouTube, reading books, tinkering with computers, applying to jobs, reading up on technology. When I started at Tyler Technologies, I wasn't completely confident, so I became a student of the job. I studied all day, every day. It wasn't about making more money, because I was on salary. It was about *understanding*.

This started to take the place of hanging out with my kids and spending time with my wife. I was always in our home office, by myself, closed off. It got to the point where the kids wouldn't even ask me for anything. They'd just go directly to their mom. In my mind, this was just a temporary thing. I thought that once I got those certifications, I'd be able to make more money, and then life would be comfortable. But after I got one certification, I had to get another one. And then another one. I started chasing certifications to the extent that I ultimately ended up with seventeen. All the while, I wasn't making any more money.

My marriage started to fall apart. Just a few months before, we had bought and built our first house from the ground up. I became the first homeowner in my family. I thought life was good. I bought my wife the house and even the Hummer she always wanted, but I wasn't putting in any quality time. We separated.

After that I was in that house, mostly alone, for what felt like forever. My kids were with me on the weekends, and I was in there by myself for the rest of the week, depressed. I was so used to the house being noisy, with the kids and the dog running around. I didn't do a lot of drinking, but there were a couple of days where I lost the will to live. I felt like I'd lost everything. I had this house, this car, and this job that *felt* like it was making me a lot of money, but my family was gone.

> **I had this house, this car, and this job that *felt* like it was making me a lot of money, but my family was gone.**

When my ex-wife found someone else, I couldn't imagine anyone else raising my kids. It hurt. But therapy is a godsend. More people should do it. In my community, it's frowned upon. I'll happily talk to any therapist, shrink, or professional with the skills to help me. It took a while for me to get over the feeling of *How could you do this to me after all I've done for you?* Gradually, I accepted that I'd been lacking as a husband by not putting in enough quality time.

Also, life happens quickly. A few months after my wife and I separated, I was at a church meetup about business and entrepreneurship, and this girl that I'd seen around a few times named Tiana came up to the microphone. She said she was a forensic accountant, traveling around the world rooting out financial fraud. I'm thinking, *Who the heck is this?* My mind was blown. I'd never heard of anything like that before.

A few days later, Valentine's Day rolled around. I was still alone in that house, and still not in the best place. It was my first Valentine's Day single since I was a teenager. I went on Facebook and messaged Tiana. *Hey, busy bee. What are you up to?* I called her "busy bee" because she was always gone, always traveling, always working. *What you got going on tonight for Valentine's Day?*

She said, "I have a date with my Xbox."

I'm thinking, *How the heck can this chick not have a date on Valentine's Day?*

I wanted to ask her out, but I already had a date lined up. I was kind of seeing someone but wasn't really feeling it. At home, I was debating whether I was even gonna go. I didn't want to be the kind of guy to flake on a girl on Valentine's Day, but I don't like leading people on either. I knew it was gonna be our last date, and went through with it. I took her on a little private plane ride over Dallas, and then we had dinner. I was messaging Tiana while I was at dinner with the other girl, which she judges me for till this day.

At Tyler Technologies, I would occasionally take liberties to work from home when I wanted to. I was otherwise in that warehouse alone all night, every night, so there was no one there to stop me. Tiana and I made a date where I'd come over with my laptop and get a little work going.

When I showed up, she asked, "Do you want a drink?"

I said sure.

Then she says, "Do you want a drink? Or do you want a *drink*?"

Then she pours all this Cîroc in my cup, and I'm thinking, *Man, this is strong.*

It was around eleven at night, and normally people didn't contact me that late. Then I got an email, which was annoying—the liquor was really starting to hit me. *Who on earth is emailing me at eleven at night? Don't come asking me for nothing, because I'm not about to do anything.*

Then, when I looked at who'd sent it, I had emailed myself. That drink hit me so hard that I had sent *myself* a screenshot of a server issue, and it was supposed to go to somebody else. At this point, Tiana took my computer, slowly pulled it away, closed it, and said, "Sir, you are done for the night."

I instantly knew that I was going to marry her. Instantly. Talking to her about her experiences, her goals, and her work ethic, I was looking at her thinking, *I've finally found the female version of myself.* She just had relentless drive and hustle. When she told me she received a full academic scholarship to Howard University and graduated with a business degree, that was the icing on the cake. So she's a genius too? Sold.

After that first date, we wanted to see each other again, but she had to go to New Orleans for work. I drove her to the airport, knowing she was gonna be there for a week. After she arrived, I texted her, "Hey, I really miss you. Would it be too creepy if I just came to where you are?"

"You mean, like, fly here?"

"Um, yeah."

"Heck yeah, come on."

The kids were only with me on the weekends, so during the week I was free to move about the country. When I got to New Orleans, her consulting firm was paying for all the accommodations. Life was good. She was on that project for a month, so I went and flew out to see her every week. By the third week, I was ready. "We haven't been together that long, but I love you, and I'm gonna marry you. I've never met anyone like you, ever."

When I proposed, we were basically chilling in bed. I was flipping through my phone, looking at rings. I showed her one and asked if she liked it. She looked for a second and said, "No, too flashy." So I went right back and kept looking, and that was it. Later, we talked about getting married sometime in the fall.

She's always been a night owl. She goes to sleep at one or two in the morning and wakes up at six, like clockwork. Around month two, she kept falling asleep around nine. Something wasn't right. Next thing you know, she's pregnant. As a result, we had to escalate our marriage timeline a bit, and I had to go talk to her dad. I showed up with a birthday gift for him and a bottle of champagne. "Happy birthday! By the way, we're pregnant, and we're getting married!"

He was cool with it, but her mom was not so happy. She kept telling her, "You don't even know this guy." She was skeptical as to whether I was going to stick around, and it took her a couple of years to learn to love me. Today, we're great.

We got married on my mom's birthday, and my dad did the ceremony. There were only five or six people there. Tiana and I both owned houses, so we decided to rent hers and move into mine. Then we went on a honeymoon to the Virgin Islands, where Tiana pushed me off a Jet Ski in the middle of the ocean to make me learn how to swim. By the time we got home, it was clear saw that she was going to play a very big part in where I was going to go.

After our honeymoon, I got right back to work. My team didn't even know I had gotten *divorced*, let alone remarried, and they found out about it on Facebook. We had another kid on the way. Again: *I gotta make more money.*

Tiana encouraged me to continue learning, and to change the way I looked at my job. "Look, they don't have you doing much. Use this as an opportunity to get paid to learn. Take care of business when you need to, and better yourself in your downtime. Get your résumé together, then get out there and into something else." That was the spark I needed to make a transition. I'm thinking, *This woman is brilliant.* My philosophy has been the same ever since: if you want a position or a promotion, you should start doing the work before it's given to you.

The next thing that happened was *very* interesting. Just as I'd been introduced to the world of security audits, I got a call from my manager. "Hey, Boyd, I need you to come into the office. We need to talk." Now, you don't have anything to be nervous about if you haven't done anything. But one of the things I *had* been doing was sneaking out of the office on Sundays to go to church. My manager and I did not see eye to eye on that, because it left our servers unsupervised. I went to his office thinking there was a fifty-fifty chance I'd be getting fired.

Then he began, "You know this PCI assessment security audit we're doing right now? It's not going very well. In fact, we're on the verge of failing. Do me a favor—go take a look in the conference room and come on back." I walked down to the conference room, and the guy that was supposed to be leading the assessment was in there snoring. Completely knocked out. His head was dangling like a rag doll. My manager asked if I could step into his position to bring things back around. *Absolutely.*

I went from the night shift to the day shift, downloaded the security framework, and just dove headfirst into the whole process. PCI stands for Payment Card Industry. It's the security standard that companies have to follow to protect credit card data, and it became my world. I completely shut out everything else and focused solely on helping the company pass our impending audit. I figured out where we were in the process, worked with the auditors, and got things to the point where we didn't fail.

When we ultimately passed the assessment, they created a security analyst position for me. I got a promotion and a pay bump, which put my salary at $76,000 a year. Doors opened for me that I wasn't aware of. I'd never traveled for business before, but security audits require physical site visits. One of the offices for Tyler Technologies was in Maine, so I had to get on the plane and fly up there. All the while, I had to take that sleepy guy with me. They never fired him—he was still there even after I quit.

The auditors we were working with noticed that I was picking everything up fast. At first, I didn't want to do what they did, because I had to teach *them* all the technical stuff. Then, after a while, I asked how much they made. They said, "$150,000." I almost hit the floor. I *immediately* changed my focus from getting certifications to learning and mastering that security framework.

I was laser focused on hitting six figures. I learned that if you're in IT and you get what's called a CISSP certification, it practically guarantees you $100,000. I was trying to stop chasing certifications for good, but *that* one I was still gonna get. I went to talk to my director. "I think it would look great to our clients if we had a CISSP on staff. It would also help me protect our systems. If you guys are willing to pay for the exam, I'll study for it on my own time, and I guarantee that I'll pass." It was a $600 exam. I was making decent money, but I still didn't want to pay for it. I studied for six weeks and passed.

After that, I went straight in and had a conversation with my senior manager. "Hey, I got this CISSP now, and $100K is the going rate." He says, "Boyd, I'm gonna be honest with you. I'm never going to be able to pay you that." Now I know I'd never make six figures working there. Thank you! *Thank you* for telling me that! Goodbye!

I updated my résumé and soon had an interview for a position in vulnerability management at American Airlines. The interview went very, very well. I came in dressed nice, smelling good, and I killed it. I had the CISSP and all the other requirements they were looking for. I had experience with the same security tool they used to do vulnerability scanning. Then, twenty minutes after that interview, I got a phone call from the recruiter. "They're not gonna go with you. They didn't feel like you had the skills necessary for the job." I forgot to ask my end-of-interview question. Shame on me.

> **I went back to the drawing board and focused on *mastering* the security framework.**

That destroyed my confidence for *years*. I was the perfect guy for that job and didn't get it. I couldn't help thinking that there was something wrong with me. For the next year and a half, I was still at Tyler Technologies, going through the motions, studying security audits. I went back to the drawing board and focused on *mastering* the security framework. The rejection from American Airlines gave me the fuel to refocus. I didn't see it then, but it eventually led me to where I am now.

Eventually, I got a call from Baylor Scott & White, one of the largest healthcare companies in Texas. I interviewed for a security engineer position, and they hired me for my PCI skills. I was only there for eight months. The company refused to invest in the resources to obtain the tools, technology, or support staff they needed to pass their audit. Because I was leading it, I would've shouldered the blame. I was thinking, *Nah, not going to be your fall guy.* So I quit. I didn't really have a choice.

I updated my profile on Dice, where IT people go to find jobs. Soon I got a phone call about a PCI architect position from a confidential company. When the recruiter listed the responsibilities the mystery company was looking for, I was like, *Oh yeah. That's me. That. Is. Me.* Then they listed all the educational qualifications required, and I'm like, *Nope, that is* not *me.* I finally just asked who the company was. Then the guy on the other line says, "American Airlines."

Crap, crap, crap. I was desperate to get out of healthcare, but now I was about to confront my old demons all over again. I interviewed for their senior security architect position, which required a command of twelve requirements and their four-hundred-plus subrequirements.

My interviewer asked me a technical question, and I came back right away: "Yeah, that happens in requirement 12.9."

He's like, "Wait, what? You know these requirements?"

"Man, I do this all day." Being able to actually recite the requirements and what they meant was the clincher. There aren't many people that can do that.

He just couldn't believe it. "How do you know this? How is that even possible? I *hate* this stuff."

"And I *love* this stuff. At the end of the day, I'm doing my service to society by making sure people's credit card information doesn't get stolen. I've been in that position, and I didn't have money to wait around to see if the bank was going to reimburse me. This is how I give back to the world."

He thought about that for a second. "You know what? I respect that."

The rest of interview went very well. And this time, I remembered to ask my final question. "Is there any reason you *wouldn't* hire me?

He replied, "If I'm being honest, I want you to go home, change, come back, and start right now." I was in a suit and tie, and they don't have that kind of dress code at American Airlines. Before I even hit the parking lot, the recruiter called me. She says, "Dude, I don't know *what* you did, but they already offered you the job."

Seventy dollars per hour. Oh, man. Yeah, buddy.

Then, immediately, the nerves kicked in. Impostor syndrome. I'm thinking, *I'm being hired as the security architect for the world's largest airline, and all I have is a high school diploma and a few years of IT behind me. What am I doing?* It was the first time I'd ever felt like that.

Tiana had to reassure me. "Boyd, I've been watching you study this stuff. Nobody knows this better than you. Why are you afraid? If you weren't right for it, they wouldn't have hired you!"

I came around. "You know what? You're right. I got this. I can do this."

Two weeks into the job, something came across my desk for approval. Guess who needed *my* approval to get some work done? The first guy that passed on me at American Airlines. Now he was reporting to *me*. Such a beautiful thing. *Such* a beautiful thing!

It was one of those times you can be an asshole or be tactful. I didn't even bring it up. I just said, "Hi, Gary. Let me get you what you need."

"Faith, family, and finances" is the mantra in our home, but unfortunately, that wasn't always the case. For too long, I was too focused on the finance portion, and it ruined my marriage and affected my children's lives. I don't want you to make the same mistake that I did. Put this book down, spend some time with your loved ones, and tell them how much they mean to you. Time is a nonreplenishing resource. Don't ever miss an opportunity to spend quality time.

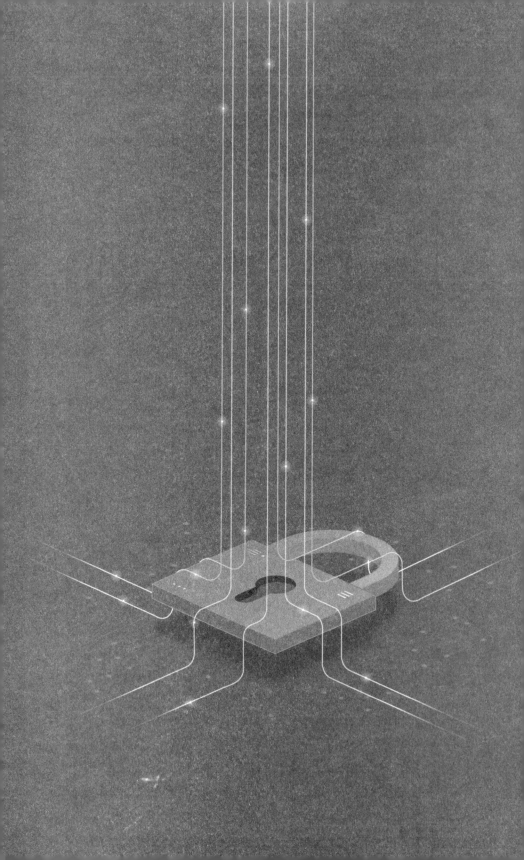

CHAPTER 5

American

American Airlines is huge and compartmentalized. I went from working at a small company to the largest airline in the world, and from 3,000 employees to over 120,000. Initially, I was overwhelmed and terrified.

As the PCI security guy at my previous companies, my core responsibility was understanding the payment transaction flow for credit card data. This typically entails three or four payment-channel types. For example, if somebody makes a payment from the internet, I had to understand how that worked. If somebody went into a medical office to make a payment at a terminal, I needed to understand how *that* works—and so on. That had always been manageable for me.

When I arrived at American Airlines, they had over *forty* different payment channels, spread across 297 airports, six international data centers, and offices in tiny countries scattered across the globe. And it was my job to understand *each and every payment flow*.

Normally, these appear on a network diagram, which is basically a blueprint for a computer network. I was used to seeing these on a simple one-page PDF. American Airlines' was so massive that they had to print it on a huge plotter and hang it on the wall. My new job was to know *everything* about it. At first, that freaked me out. AA.com is one of the biggest websites in the world. Their minute-by-minute traffic is *crazy*.

Jay, the guy that I was replacing, had accepted a position at another company as a chief information and security officer (CISO), a pretty big promotion. Fortunately for me, he and Ali, the guy that hired me, had a great relationship. Ali arranged an after-work meeting for Jay to walk me through the entire process. Jay was knowledgeable and shy. When I asked to record our talk to study later, he immediately got nervous. I had to beg him a little and promise I wouldn't share it with anyone.

I called Tiana, told her I'd be home late, and ordered some of the surprisingly good burritos from the gas station up the street. Then we sat there for three straight hours going over that huge network diagram. Jay walked me through everything, gave me the inside and out on the different departments and personalities involved, and generally showed me how to approach things.

After that, my confidence went through the roof. I came into the job solid from a security-standard standpoint, but now I was applying that knowledge to a significantly more complicated environment. With Jay's help, everything that had been so intimidating three hours before suddenly seemed manageable. Had he not laid things out for me so clearly, I don't know what I would have done.

When I look back at my first weeks at American Airlines, it still gives me chills. Going from having no formal education and struggling financially to overseeing this giant network was an amazing feeling. I went in with an early version of what I now call the Authority Mindset: I'm going to be the best at whatever it is I do, and I'm going to put in the work required to be an expert. If I'm going to be involved, you're going to get all of me. I went straight on the offensive. I wasn't waiting for assignments to be handed to me.

Once I understood how the payment network worked, we had two months until the audit. I started making phone calls, sending emails, asking people for meetings, and gathering evidence. I wanted to eliminate any potential issues *before* the auditors rolled up. I was also basically out there shaking hands and kissing babies. A lot of the employees at American Airlines hadn't spoken with anyone with my level of knowledge about security frameworks. In giving a wide variety of people implementation advice to ease the burden of the audit, my consulting skills started to blossom.

My job was essentially to act as an internal consultant. American Airlines' different business units are so compartmentalized that it was basically like dealing with many different businesses inside of one company. There are different states and countries, different business types, and different operations, but they all fall under the same security standard. I had to act as the bearer of the Rosetta stone between all those different links.

I started traveling extensively and had to learn cultural differences on the fly. On my first trip to Argentina, I reached out to shake hands with an office manager there. She looked at my hand like *Um, we don't do that here,* then brought me in and kissed me on the cheek. Later, I had a meeting with the VP of Panasonic, who had flown in from Japan. He bowed reverentially as he presented me his business card, and then I just nonchalantly took it from him. Apparently, that's disrespectful. He didn't appear to be offended, but afterward one of my colleagues had to lean in and whisper to me, "Hey, when they give you their business card, it's like they're giving you a part of themselves. It's a very important moment, so you need to receive it the same way."

Now I'm very mindful of things like that. Things like this prepared me more and more for building an international presence.

———————————— 🔒 ————————————

I would be lying if I said it was all rosy. Growing up, I didn't feel like I was good at a lot of things. My brother was this superstar linebacker, and my sister was a great athlete and lifelong straight-A student. I lived in my brother's shadow throughout high school. Most of my former classmates probably only recently found out what my actual name is because of the press I've been getting. Back then, I was known as Will's brother or Little Clew.

At American Airlines, I was finally in a place where I was The Man, where I had my own name. Initially, I built up some arrogance around that, and when management wanted to take the easy way out, it didn't always go well. I hadn't developed the tact to have conversations at that level, so I ended up in some pretty heated arguments with leadership about direction. Not everyone was my friend. I was audacious enough to tell people senior to me when I didn't like their tone. "I understand that you're old enough to be my dad, but you're not gonna talk to me like that." This is me at twenty-five, talking to a fifty-year-old CISO three levels above me!

> **I hadn't developed the tact to have conversations at that level, so I ended up in some pretty heated arguments with leadership about direction.**

My immaturity ultimately made my job more difficult. I was on a team of four people. When the CISO I talked back to would come over to our cubicles, he would engage my three teammates and ignore me—wouldn't make eye contact, acted like I didn't exist. He would say things behind my back but never to my face. I have trouble respecting people who do that. Anything I would say behind your back, I would say to your face. That's just the kind of person I am.

Now that I'm older and thinking clearly, it's like, "What were you *thinking*?" But at the time, I *know* what I was thinking: *they can't replace me.* I knew they'd never find anybody that knew the network and standards like me. And for that reason, I got away with a lot. I quit in 2018, and they *still* haven't replaced me.

The argument with my CISO came up with my and Tiana's marriage counselor. Around the same time, Tiana and I had gotten in a fight about something trivial. I got upset, grabbed a pot, and threw it across the room. The situation did not deserve that type of response, to say the least. It also wasn't the first time that I had gotten highly upset about something that wasn't that big of a deal. Our marriage counselor recommended that I get tested for bipolarity.

At the time, even that suggestion rubbed me the wrong way. I know I'm a Sour Patch Kid, but bipolar? I scheduled an appointment with a psychiatrist as recommended, did the test, and it turns out that I *am* bipolar.

I was immediately thinking, *This really changes things.* Right away, they were telling me to take medications that I would have to continue taking for the rest of my life. The second thing I was thinking was, *How long have I been dealing with this? How many relationships and opportunities have I destroyed because of this thing that I didn't even know about?* I thought having a short temper was just part of my personality, not a full-on disorder. I started thinking about some of the things I did in in high school. One of the side effects of bipolarity is sexual impulsivity. Is that why I had so much girl trouble? Back when I was with Ashlee, I had punched through our microwave. Who punches through a microwave? It was a hard pill to swallow.

I could only imagine how Tiana was feeling. When we talked about it, she was relieved—at least there was a path forward and it was something we could manage. But for a while, I was pretty down in the dumps about the diagnosis. I felt like I was disabled, and that hit my confidence a bit. I felt like I was this smart IT guy, finally doing well, and now I have this *disorder*. There's stigma around bipolarity. In Texas, people are always talking about the bipolar weather. It seemed negative, and I didn't want to tell anybody about it. For a while, I carried around a lot of shame.

There's lots of mental illness on my dad's side of the family: there was a schizophrenic uncle, a bipolar aunt, and his mom and another uncle were mentally disabled. Four out of seven children had significant mental disorders that were severe enough that they couldn't get jobs. I grew up seeing that, so I have a level of respect for people with mental disabilities. People aren't often given the respect they're due, and many are cast aside.

Until we lose the negative stigma around mental disorders, people dealing with them will just have to find the power that can come from them. You can still be successful, but it took me years. With bipolarity, one of the things that comes with the territory is officially called "thoughts of grandeur," or what I would simply call *wild ideas*. More and more, that got me thinking about the wild ideas I had when I was younger.

Years later, when I dreamed up my current business, right away I was hoping to change lives and make millions of dollars. I could instantly see the path forward and exactly how I would do it. Now I see this line of thought through a new lens. To some extent, my entire business was birthed from a manic episode.

Of course, there's nothing wrong with having big ideas. But what I learned is that you also need a support system—someone to run ideas by so you don't make foolish decisions. When you're in the high of a manic episode, everything just feels right. You need somebody in your corner to tell you *No, actually, that doesn't make sense*. And they need to legitimately have your best interests in mind, instead of potentially imposing their own limitations on you.

When I started taking the medicine I was prescribed, I didn't know how it would affect me. I scheduled a meeting with my manager at American to fill him in on everything, and he was as supportive as anyone could be. The first week was pretty rocky. The medicine made me sleepy. I had so much work to do and initially struggled to accomplish it. There was a Starbucks inside the corporate office, so I was down there every morning getting my tall white mocha, no whipped cream. By lunchtime, I'd be drained. For the rest of my tenure, every day I'd have to go to my car in the parking garage, push the seats out of the way, climb in the back, get the air conditioning pumping, put my blazer over my head, and take a forty-five-minute nap.

Eventually, despite everything, I got into a groove at American Airlines. One of the hard things about my position was that I could tell people *what* to do, but I couldn't *make* anyone do anything. Sometimes you need that executive push, like when someone's not delivering on time. Plus, security is not something that people want to do. Think about your phone or computer. How often do you rotate your passwords? We had a framework that mandated rotating our passwords every thirty days. They had to be a specific number of characters, go through multifactor authentication, and pair with individual phone tokens. It goes on and on.

People weren't really trying to hear all this, but I didn't care. I take what I do seriously. I understood the legal implications and the potential impact for clients. Without the proper controls in place, we could get breached. If we got breached, then our customers would be affected, and their credit card data could be stolen and used all around the world. Then I'd be out of a job. This was constantly in my mind while making decisions. Balancing budget and time constraints forced me to get extra creative with solving problems. I eventually got a new nickname: the human compensating control. I was always talking my way out of issues with security auditors.

I also developed a reputation for telling people no. It got so bad that people started bypassing me and going straight to production with their ideas, because they already knew what I was gonna say. After a year or so of this, I had to sit down and think. *Why would they do this? Don't they understand risk?* My core problem was that I was thinking like an IT person. IT people generally don't become successful business owners because they're so focused on technology. IT *security*, on the other hand, is a top-level function of *business*. You don't have much of a choice in making sure your business operates securely.

Instead of telling people no, what I should have been saying was, *No, not* that *way—let's figure out a way to do this securely so you can get your job done.* When I made that switch, my reputation changed. I wish that I had done so from the get-go, but it was a learning experience. Now this is something I teach my students. The name of the game is *business enablement.* If people are looking at you as a business *hindrance*, they'll avoid you at all costs.

The moment things really shifted for me was when the company wanted to move our payment processing out of our data center and into the cloud. My initial response: *Absolutely not.* I just immediately thought about the risks. *We're taking something in-house that's verified, secure, and functions properly and moving it all to the cloud?* When I read their initial email, it was like, *nope!* I thought I'd shut them down, and it'd be a quick meeting.

Then, they rolled in with backup. They brought in the vendor, who anticipated my reservations. When we had a conversation, I learned right away that they weren't just doing it to do it. The business reasons behind it were sound. First, it would make for faster payment processing. Second, we wouldn't have to store credit card data anymore. Not having to store millions of customer credit cards dramatically reduced our risk. Third, it also lessened the burden on our inevitable security audit, because they were using a prevalidated payment processor that had already gone through a security assessment.

The person managing this project was so well organized, and her business case was clear, cut and dry. The people I had brushed off before weren't as clear, so it was easier for me to tell them no. This time, when I reconsidered my initial knee-jerk opinion, a light bulb went off in my head. I started asking myself, *How many other ideas have you just blown off?* All my life, after I had formulated an opinion on something or someone, for many people I'd be like talking to a brick wall.

I realized that that mentality had been doing me more harm than good. I needed to be more flexible and open to listening. I started changing the way that I communicated with *everyone.* Before, if one of my kids' teachers sent me an email about that something happened at school, that was that—I didn't really want to hear what my kids had to say. As I started to change, it became, "All right. Here's what the teacher said. Now let me hear *your* side of the story."

I ended up having to put this into practice right away. One morning I got a calendar invite for a meeting to discuss a new initiative: American was giving out virtual credit cards. They were basically gift certificates for people who had been inconvenienced by flight delays. Initially I was thinking they were just indiscriminately sending out credit cards, and alarms were going off in my head left and right.

But this time, I checked myself: *Come into this with an open mind. Let's hear what they have to say.* They walked me through the process. All they were really doing was generating prepaid credit card numbers that were good for fifty dollars. The same way that they would print a boarding pass, they would print out these "credit cards" on paper, which airport vendors were set up to accept as payment. It was weird, but it worked. When I looked at the overall risk, it wasn't very high. I'm thinking, *Okay, this makes sense.* It allowed the airline to feed customers who were stuck at the airport. Even I benefited from it once when I got stuck in Miami. From then on, my working relationships ran far smoother.

My biggest win at AA came out of left field. Our auditors would hit ten or fifteen airports every year, and my job was to be one step ahead of them. While making sure everything was in order for them, I wound up talking to a gate agent who took me through her process. I was asking her very basic questions. Before I started working at AA, I still hadn't done a lot of traveling, so a lot of the steps involved were still foreign to me.

She showed me one of the receipts that were printed after each purchase, and I noticed that it had a full credit card number on it, complete with expiration date. A year before, I would have completely freaked out, but by now I was cool, calm, and collected. "Okay, okay. This *could* be a problem. Can you help me understand what you're doing with all these receipts?"

She opened a drawer, and there were stacks and stacks of the receipts in there, all from that day. When I asked where the rest were, she walked me to a back office and showed me a locked filing cabinet overflowing with more.

They were printing out two receipts for every purchase: one for the customer and one for AA. Then, at the end of the night, the shift manager would spend two or three hours auditing them. When they were done, they put all the receipts into a huge bag, duct-taped it shut, put a red seal on it, threw it onto a conveyor belt, and shipped the receipts to Juarez to be destroyed.

When I came back home, I found the person who managed this whole process. I introduced myself and posed a simple question: *Is there any particular reason as to why we're printing out the full credit card number?* She had no idea. "It's just always been like that."

I went back to my desk to sit and ponder this for a moment. I contemplated the costs: 297 airports, times two to three hours a day auditing receipts, plus shipping reams of paper to Mexico, and then paying a company to destroy them.

American was paying this company somewhere around half a million dollars a year *just to destroy receipts*. For the next few days, I couldn't stop thinking about it.

Whoever was destroying the receipts had access to bags and bags of our credit card data, which could affect our security assessment. That officially made the situation my purview, which granted me access to the contract. When I checked it out, American was paying this company somewhere around half a million dollars a year *just to destroy receipts*. For the next few days, I couldn't stop thinking about it.

I started doing more research and looked more deeply into our gate agent software. I immediately noticed that the way they had to enter their usernames and passwords was *also* insecure. Now I had two big issues on my hands, and if the security auditors found out about either, we'd fail our assessment.

I set up a meeting with my manager, the director of applications. She was completely unaware. By the end of our meeting, she was looking at me like a deer in the headlights. We went back to the drawing board and concluded it would take eight weeks to get everything on track, and she put me in charge of a team to knock it out. We ultimately axed the nightly audit process and the printing of all those receipts.

As my résumé *still* puts it, I had "reclaimed over 56,000 hours of annual employee time and an annual savings of $500,000+ by designing new functionality to eliminate the storage, transportation, and destruction of paper containing credit card data."

From that point forward, I was like American's IT security rock star, and I'd barely been there a year. Whenever something came up related to PCI, credit cards, or data security, people were calling me. I was getting flown out all over the place to do presentations for different business units, helping people come up with compliance strategies. At one point, even the résumé of that sleepy guy from back at Tyler Technologies came across my desk. That was a hard no.

A few months later, American won a big industry award for ranking the number-one airline in the industry. The CEO decided to celebrate by giving every employee two free round-trip tickets anywhere in the world. Right away, I called Tiana. She always wanted to see the Sydney Opera House, so we decided to go for her birthday.

During our layover at LAX, we were sitting at the gate, dreading the fifteen-hour flight. I turned to her like, "Hey, I have an idea. Let's just go over to the bar and have some drinks. Then we'll be nice and relaxed, and we can get on the plane and go to sleep." I was saying it all nice, but I really just wanted to get drunk so I could pass out for as much of the flight as I could.

As we're sitting at the bar drinking mimosas, I heard, "Boyd Clewis! Recheck!" over the loudspeaker.

That usually meant bad news. Whenever you're traveling as an employee of American Airlines, you're what they call "non rev," or nonrevenue, so whenever a flight is overbooked, you're the first person they kick off the plane. At first I was like, *Nope, not getting up. I'm sipping my drink in peace.* But eventually Tiana made me go see what was up.

I walked up to the counter, and the lady working there handed me a pair of tickets like a precious gift. I looked down: first class. In shock, I slowly turned and gave them to Tiana. I didn't have the words. I had flown first class before on regular planes, but I had never flown first class like *this.* I still don't know how it happened. Those tickets cost thirty grand *each way.*

We *ran* onto the plane, not knowing what to expect—I just knew I wasn't gonna be in coach for fifteen hours. They handed us bags with pajamas, toothbrushes, slippers, headphones, pillows, and blankets. The seats just rolled out into beds. After takeoff, we were eating salmon and caviar—that was the first and last time I've ever had caviar. Right away they're asking, "Would you like a drink, sir?" I'm like, *Yes, absolutely. More drinks.*

Statistically speaking, not everyone will be diagnosed with a mental illness, but everyone should still take steps to maintain mental health. My challenge for you: Create a mental health routine. It could consist of daily meditation, speaking with a counselor, or something as simple as a morning walk.

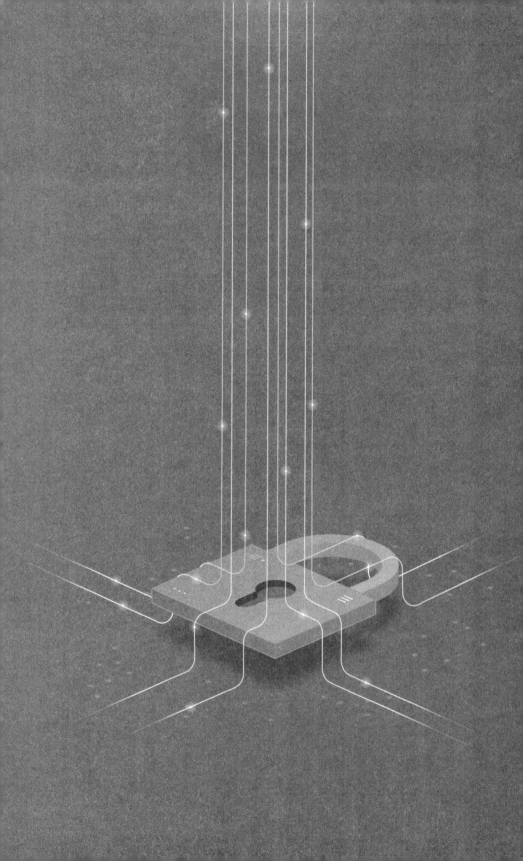

CHAPTER 6

Sherlock Homey

When we got back, I continued traveling around and connecting with other people in the payment security industry, especially by speaking at conferences. The first time I ever attended the biggest conference for cyber and payment security—the PCI Community Meeting—I couldn't help thinking, *One day, I'm gonna speak on this stage.* It's put on by the people who oversee the entire industry, and all the biggest companies come in from all over the world: Visa, MasterCard, American Express, you name it. Anyone that processes payments via credit card at a high level has to be there. The first of many I attended was in Barcelona, and there, during an little intermission, I snuck up onto the stage to take a picture. I could just see it happening.

I was doing a ton of networking. I approached one of the keynote speakers, Harvey Roberts, and told him how much I liked his presentation. He was delighted, because he didn't think it went over well. Everyone was wearing name tags, and he looked down at mine and said, "Ah, Boyd Clewis, American Airlines—I've heard about you."

I'm like, "Really?!"

"I heard you're a good consultant. You should come over to the dark side"—in other words, become an auditor myself.

Right away I told him, "Nah, nah. I can't. I have four kids. Too much travel." In that job, at any given time you may have to jump on the plane out of the country for as long as they need you.

He said, "I get it. But if and when your situation changes, let me know."

Back at work, I was taking my obsession with the PCI security standard to really create a new direction for my career. I just focused relentlessly on adding massive value. I put on training clinics for American, was booking out conference rooms for a week at a time and doing eight-hour training classes for employees from all over the world. At the end of the week, my throat would hurt from talking all day. I was just trying to make sure that everybody understood exactly what they needed to do to maintain compliance and let everyone know what the impact could be if we didn't.

No one told me to do any of this, and I didn't sit around and wait for work to come to me. I had to light fires under people. Today, as an auditor, I can't fix other people's problems—I can only tell them what to do. But my work made the audits easier on everyone and saved us money. I streamlined processes for doing airport security assessments. I trained airport management so they could train *their* staff. PCI assessments took twelve months when I got to American. By the time I left, we were wrapping them up in seven.

I wasn't able to do any of this on my own. I wholeheartedly believe in helping people win, putting yourself in the position to win by helping those around you to become better. Look at Kobe Bryant and the 2010 Lakers. They won the championship because Kobe made them better, and I took that as inspiration. I was on the team with four people, and I spent individual time with them every day, giving them insights that helped them do their jobs better. Eventually, when a task came my way, I could pass those things to them with the confidence that they would do a good job.

Instead of just giving out answers, I would teach people to think through the process and come up with their own solution. I'd rather teach someone how to think than give them the answer. I built a strong team, and that's partly why they still haven't had to replace me. They begged me to stay, but the core people that I placed there are so good that they don't need me.

More doors opened. I spoke at the American Airlines Security Conference, sharing billing with the CISOs for the states of Texas and Arizona. Soon, the PCI Community Meeting rolled back around. This time, it was in Vegas, and Harvey Roberts was speaking again. He invited me over to a little after-hours event at a bar. By this time, I was ready to leave American Airlines. He said his year-old offer was still on the table. When I talked to Tiana, she said to take it but to make sure we could still afford to travel without all the free plane tickets we'd been getting from American. I told him I needed $200K, and he said he could make it happen. I was nonchalant and straight faced with him but completely losing it inside. $200,000!

I wanted to take some time off between American and my new employer. Then, almost right away, they called me needing a security assessment for a bank in Dallas. They wanted me to lead an NCSF assessment, which I knew nothing about. They were not only asking me to start early but to lead my very first assessment in a completely new framework in seven days. You know what my response was? *Of course. This is what I do.*

I rolled up my sleeves. The NCSF is a government assessment, so there were all sorts of free resources available online. In the end, it was similar to the PCI standard I was already used to. I conducted this new assessment in essentially the same way but with slightly different questions. It didn't even take the whole week. When it came time to meet with the bank, the assessment went through flawlessly—no issues whatsoever. I was extremely nervous at first, but after that it was a very easy transition for me.

I had never done consulting, but Tiana was deeply in that world and coached me through the process. The transition would not have been nearly as easy without her. I didn't know anybody else in this line of work. She taught me how to coordinate travel, bookkeeping, expense accounts, setting expectations, managing time. You have to be extremely organized, which was a challenge for my scattered, bipolar brain. Consulting is just a different beast.

One of the things I learned immediately: Ask for everything that you want up front, because once you're in there, they've got you. I got stuck with a crappy Windows PC, even though I'm a Mac guy—I could've asked for a top-of-the-line Mac up front, and I'm sure I would've gotten it. I also had to realize that the company that you work for is not really paying you. Your *clients* are paying you, and they're paying you for your time. Instead of working forty hours a week, I had quotas for billable hours. I was working with ten to fifteen different clients, sometimes all in the same week. When you work for a consulting firm, you're essentially a business owner. Your company is just bringing in the clients, and it's up to you to manage those relationships.

In consulting, deliverables are everything, and they're all laid out in your contract: *this is what will be delivered, by this time, after this many hours.* If you're not organized, you can get a hundred hours into a project and realize it's going to take twenty extra. Then you're in trouble—at $250 or $500 an hour, billing twenty extra hours isn't a small deal. I had to learn my way around that fast. Before, I was able to skate by in my career without having that kind of tight structure, and I had to establish it as a consultant quickly. Fortunately, my wife is the most organized person I've ever met in my life. She almost singlehandedly taught me self-management, which is so, so important for success.

Once I got the hang of it, I had never experienced such freedom in my life. My home became my office. I got up in the morning and could decide whether I was gonna put on grown-people clothes or not. I wish I would've found that kind of freedom sooner, but I needed the experience at American Airlines to get there. I was providing security services for some of the largest, household-name companies in the world. It was hard to believe these huge players were coming to me for my expertise.

By this point, it was more and more about playing the game. I was starting to have a good understanding of what makes people sign deals in the world of business. Most IT people are focused on the wrong thing. Most of them think like I used to, and spend their time chasing certifications. They think those certifications will make them more money because their employers will see them as more valuable.

That, my friends, is a fallacy. What *will* make you more money is one of two things: making the company *more* money or helping the company offset the risk of *losing* money. It's about money, not technology. IT is about the value you bring to the table and the size of the problems you solve.

If you want to get paid well, you need to solve big problems. There are millions of people who can fix computers and therefore, it's not a big problem. At American Airlines, there were 120,000 employees and 100,000 devices. One computer doesn't stop the show. But if the *company* fails a security assessment needed to process credit card payments or maintain contracts with other service providers, or could potentially shut down a website that makes approximately $80 million a day—if you can manage that, *now* you're bringing real *value* to the table.

Somewhere along the line, I realized that I needed to look at my career as if I were a doctor. I used to love watching *Nip/Tuck*. Those plastic surgeons were making *so* much money, and it wasn't because they were the greatest at their jobs. It's because they specialized in something that people deemed important. Generalists don't get paid like specialists, because specialists don't solve the same kinds of problems. The plastic surgeon is gonna get paid a heck of a lot more than a general doctor, just like an electrician is gonna get paid more than a general contractor. Jack must die. If you're a jack-of-all-trades, you're a master of none. I could do everything when it came to IT, but when I got into the PCI thing, Jack died. I focused on one thing and became a master.

I branched out and started building an international brand as a speaker and consultant. That first time I attended the PCI Community Meeting, I had also noticed right away that some of the speakers were not polished. At the back of my mind, I couldn't help thinking, *I can do better.* When I had left American and increasingly started flying around the world, consulting, and making contacts, more and more people liked the way I conducted business. That ultimately got me an invite to speak for the PCI Standards Council.

Having to come up with an idea for a presentation made me realize how much my experience as a system administrator and IT support guy helped me as a security consultant. Some of the lazy practices that I picked up as an admin are a security person's nightmares: sharing passwords, using one password for an entire team, not installing system updates, etcetera. I knew where to check myself because I had *been* that guy.

I had to get creative when brainstorming what to do for the presentation. The idea was to do a live demo of someone stealing credit card data from a system in a way that mirrored real life. It happens all the time: an administrator shares account info insecurely, it falls into the wrong hands, data gets stolen, and we can't determine the guilty party—the administrators don't want to be held responsible, so they're never honest, and then everyone's pointing the finger at everyone else. It's just like siblings when something gets broken in the house and the parents get mad—nobody's guilty.

I turned that whole situation into a mystery and wanted to engage the audience by having them solve it. Instead of a whodunit, I called it a "Su-Dunnit." It's a geeky in-joke: on Linux systems, whenever you're operating at the highest access level, that level is called *sudo*. I went and bought a Sherlock Holmes hat and a pipe at Party City, and eventually introduced myself as Sherlock Homey. That made me *so much money*, because it made me recognizable. One of my current employees calls me Sherlock to this day.

I flew out to Vancouver for the week and walked into the auditorium before presenting. The whole setup was breathtaking. Thousands of people were going to be in attendance. Even before I spoke, I realized, *This is it. This is really happening.* They gave me a speaker badge, and I then had to get makeup done for the first time.

I still remember telling this lady backstage, "You are *not* about to put makeup on me."

She showed me a horrible picture of someone without stage makeup and said, "Well, this is how you'll look on stage if you go without it."

That changed my mind immediately. "Okay. Fine. Shine me up."

There were three thousand people inside of the arena, and thousands more streaming, but I felt comfortable from all the presentations I'd done at American. I'd sat in boardrooms with leadership and multimillionaire-CEO-type people. I wasn't nervous at all. I felt like I belonged because I had put in the work. I knew I was an expert in what I was talking about, and that gave me confidence.

It also helped that back at American, they offered free intensive training for all kinds of things, including what was normally a very expensive course called Presentation Advantage. They walked us through the elements of how to craft presentations, how to make them look good, how to speak well, how to deliver, and all the rest. Going through that boosted my confidence. We had to get up, put a presentation together, and give it in front of the class. When we were graded by the instructor and our peers, I got great feedback right away. And they weren't just giving out participation trophies—some of the people in there were just horrible. After that I was thinking, *Maybe there's something to this.*

The other crucial thing was developing an alter ego. Boyd's an introvert who's perfectly fine being alone. But when it's time to hit the stage, that's when Mr. Clewis comes out, and he's a completely different guy. I step on the stage, the lights hit me, and I transform. Something shifts when I get onstage.

Then, when I'm done, I don't remember anything at all. Before I start a presentation, I still tell people: "Make sure you're taking notes. I might say something profound, and chances are I won't remember it." Something else just takes over. It has to. You have to bring a certain kind of superhuman energy. You can't be droning on, putting everybody to sleep.

As an introvert, it takes so much energy to be in a room with a lot of people. After the presentation, I went back and hid out in the greenroom. My coworkers came back there like, "Boyd! Come on!

> **Before I start a presentation, I still tell people: "Make sure you're taking notes. I might say something profound, and chances are I won't remember it."**

There's a party going on!" I'm like, "Cool, I'll catch up with you guys."

Nope, not at all. I just sat there in the greenroom until everyone cleared out, sat in the lobby looking out at the Vancouver skyline, and had a moment of reflection. I finally did it, and it went well. After everyone left the party, I snuck back in, grabbed a bunch of the leftover hors d'oeuvres, and went straight back to my Airbnb.

As I started to understand consulting more, I had to shake myself out of that introversion, because I was ruining my moneymaker. When you're speaking at an event and you do a good job, you're instantly influential. People want to talk to you. And when people want to talk to you, they'll usually pay you to help them. Speaking turns into consulting deals.

I was beating myself up over not putting myself out there for a while, thinking about how many deals I didn't land as a result. I just had to man up. I figured that if I could turn the alter ego on to get on stage, I could keep the alter ego on to hold conversations afterward.

You gotta do uncomfortable things to get to where you want to go. Once you do it enough, you can actually find your zone of genius and get comfortable. Some people don't believe they can be good at something that they're uncomfortable with. When I first started public speaking, I was good at it, but I was still extremely uncomfortable. Through repetition, being intentional about why I was doing it, and turning on that alter ego, I became more and more at ease. It really comes down to training your mind to believe. Belief is a powerful drug. Think about drug trials, and how so many people end up healing themselves when all they're taking is placebos.

Creating an alter ego is no different. You have to choose one that's meaningful to you. When people ask who my favorite superhero is, I tell them it's Batman, hands-down. I like to think of myself as Bruce Wayne. Boyd is Bruce Wayne; Mr. Clewis is Batman. When I travel, I rent exotic cars. When I touch down somewhere, I always spring for the Lamborghini or Ferrari, because I'm Bruce Wayne, you know what I mean? Bruce Wayne's not gonna pull up in a Honda Civic.

I transform when I need to, and that helps me to take the pressure off Boyd. I can use that alter ego to transfer the stress. You can dress it up with a costume, but at a deeper level, it's about flipping a switch and thinking differently. When I'm on stage, I'm not actively thinking as Boyd. I'm operating in what I can only call a zone of genius.

Another thing I had to learn: don't leave your alter ego in other people's hands. Not everyone will agree with your methodology or how you're trying to advance yourself. You can't let that dictate what you do. Some people would say that I'm not qualified to speak on the stages that I do. That's just their opinion, and frankly, I don't care. Other people's opinions aren't gonna stop me from doing what I do. If you let other people's words into your mind, they can start affecting you in a way that's all out of proportion. Subconsciously, it can lead you to start doubting yourself. Don't let that happen.

Whenever I'm speaking, I still try to get access to the venue a few hours before I go on, stand in the spot where I'm gonna speak, close my eyes, and just visualize everyone reacting positively. I call it channeling. In a sense, I've been doing it at least since that first trip to Barcelona in 2013, years before making any of this happen.

Do what you love. One of the biggest lessons I learned from my career is to chase after your passion. I spent years "working" until I decided to go all in on the PCI DSS framework. I ended up enjoying what I did so much that it didn't feel like work.

Let's find your passion. Here's what I want you to do:

Make a Career History: Brain dump all the jobs and positions that you've had in the past, including all paid, volunteer, and internship positions.

Favorite Career Attributes: Make a list of at least ten attributes from your previous positions that you'd like to see in your next career. This can be anything: type of work performed, team structure, commute, industry, travel, perks—whatever you want.

Least Favorite Career Attributes: Make a list of at least ten attributes from your previous positions that you would **not** like to see in your next career.

Career Deal Breakers: From your previous list of least favorite career attributes, make a list of five that you consider complete deal breakers.

Future Career Attributes: Brain dump any additional attributes that you would like to see in your ideal career path that you haven't yet experienced. Once again, it can be anything.

When you put all this together, you should have a clearer picture of a career path that's aligned with your passion.

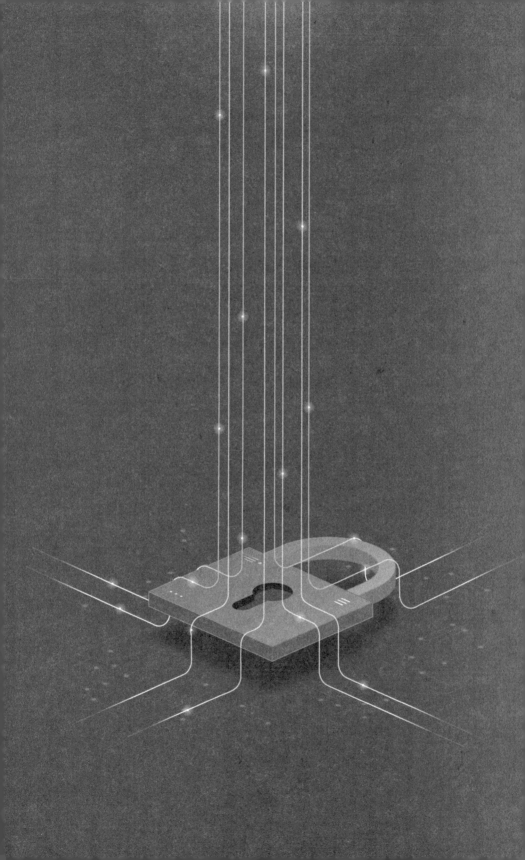

CHAPTER 7

Baxter Clewis I—Creation

I was promoted as a consultant within six months. Suddenly I was managing five other security consultants and immediately needed to hire two more. Although each position was paying a $150,000 base salary, as hard as I tried, I could not find anybody to fill them. PCI is so specialized. It's hard to find people that can actually do the job. I checked my network and reached out to people, and nobody had the skills. Before long I was thinking, *You know what? I'm gonna start a training academy.*

I knew I could strike gold. There was nobody out there training people in PCI. Right away, I wanted to figure out how to put people in high-paying jobs that didn't require certifications or college degrees. I took it upon myself to leverage my network and influence to start building that business while I was still working as a consultant. Part of this had even been gestating since doing those eight-hour seminars for American Airlines.

I already had plenty of practice in distilling my knowledge into something comprehensive and comprehensible, then conveying it to people from scratch. As soon as the idea of creating my own program came to mind, I was sleeping four hours a night for three weeks straight. I was still on my meds, but they're not foolproof. Making the dream a reality turned into one big manic episode.

I would get up at seven in the morning, take the kids to school, consult during regular working hours, build out my program until four in the morning, take a nap, and repeat. I stayed up all night for four or five days recording my first videos. As technology director of our church, I had the keys and access to all the equipment, so I'd be in there alone at 3:00 a.m. setting up cameras.

My initial idea was to start a company and call it Security Consulting Online. The idea was to help IT professionals become security consultants. I recorded a bunch of videos and started trying to market them as a thousand-dollar twelve-week program. Looking back, it was crazy to sell *three months* of my time for a thousand dollars.

When I put everything online, nothing happened. I started putting out gimmicky social media ads, and it didn't help. Admittedly, the quality of my content was trash. The cameras at church were good, but I had bought a thirty-dollar microphone from Amazon and was recording through Zoom. Somehow, amazingly, I still managed to hook three people, but one asked for a refund and the other two dropped off the face of the earth.

The audio/visual quality was one of the reasons why my first client asked for a refund. "I paid a thousand dollars for *this*? I expected more." That just crushed me, because I knew I was capable of better. I'd never created a course before. But I also had a sense that something deeper wasn't right, and that I'd have to come at it from a different angle.

Sometimes you don't know what you don't know. And what I *still* didn't know, even after my lack of success going door-to-door back in my days as the Computer Doctor, was that I just flat-out did not understand marketing. I could deliver on teaching, but I wasn't clearly broadcasting the result that I was going to provide to my students.

So, what did I do? Number one, I did not give up. I still had my cybersecurity consultant gig going on, traveling extensively. All the while, I couldn't get the idea of this program out of my head. I started making casual videos of all the cool stuff I was doing: walking through the futuristic airport in Qatar, flying in a $25,000 first-class seat with a bed and a bar, not paying for any of it. When I started sharing that kind of material, people started coming at me. Something clicked. People were basically asking, "Dude, how are you doing this?"

Every day I spent hours and hours learning about what my ideal customers wanted and where they were.

Everything was still marinating. I resolved to do more organic marketing and started doing a crazy amount of research. I obsessively dissected other business courses, studied their ads, and stalked the people that commented on their posts—especially the positive ones. I slowly became an expert in the people who bought and went through courses like mine. I read their profiles and investigated their interests. What kind of posts were they making? What type of shows do they like? How old are they? Where do they live? Every day I spent hours and hours learning about what my ideal customers wanted and where they were.

After my first failed launch, I also realized that I couldn't do everything by myself. I had to bring Tiana into the mix. Again, she's just so organized. When it comes to processes and structure, you can bring her something chaotic, and she'll get it streamlined and organized. I needed that, because I'm very conceptual. I can come up with the crazy ideas, but I need help on the back-end structure to make everything happen.

I also shifted my focus away from training people to become consultants and into getting IT professionals into the cybersecurity space. I renamed my program the Boyd Clewis Training Academy. I still had $2,000 to reinvest from the two people who didn't demand refunds from my original course, so I bought better equipment. I recorded more lessons, found a new platform to host the course, and started marketing it.

This time around, my pricing structure wasn't much better. I opened the program up for $1 for the first month and $47 per month thereafter. That gave people access to all my online training, and people *still* weren't biting. I had five or six people take me up on the one-dollar first month; then they all canceled before the next month kicked in.

I had spent hours and hours building this program for what felt like nothing. But I ultimately learned something from the experience that I will take to my grave: sell it before you build it. If the market doesn't want what you're selling, then you've wasted your time building it. Time is something that you never get back, and I wasted weeks of mine putting together a program that nobody wanted. I obviously believed it was good, but my *audience* didn't. It was a very, very tough lesson to learn.

I tried selling it in different ways and kept changing my marketing tactics, and still, nothing seemed to work. I was simply not connecting with my prospects at all. In the end, it doesn't matter how good your product is. If you can't market it, you won't sell it. After all this time, I *still* didn't realize that I fundamentally had a marketing problem.

I knew I had a product that could change lives, but I couldn't get anything to happen. I talked to my brother about how frustrated I was. By this time, he was becoming a mindset guru and performance coach. His original side hustle was running a gym—he started it on the side as a middle school teacher, quit his job, went full time, and became very successful.

I can't overstate the significance of seeing someone close to me do that. He didn't go to business school. He has a bachelor's degree, but he was a football player and did the bare minimum to get it. In his case, it didn't matter—just like it ultimately wouldn't in mine. The main thing he taught me was that I didn't need to depend on anybody else to provide for my family. He knew that I had what it took to leave my nine-to-five and do well on my own, degree or not. Seeing him do it before me gave me the confidence that I could make it happen too.

He suggested we get away for a day to figure everything out. We went to Rockwell, a little city outside Dallas, checked in at a resort on the lake there, and immediately got to work. This was all in the peak of COVID-19, and everyone was still pretty paranoid. I was mostly at peace with it, but Will wasn't. He came in with a huge bottle of Lysol and sprayed down the whole room. I'm like, "You don't have to do that, man. This is the Hilton. They already did that for us before we got here." He was looking at me like I'm crazy, spraying Lysol everywhere like, "Shit, I ain't taking no chances."

We were going nonstop, talking back and forth, brain and heart dumping. I ultimately didn't get a whole lot of sleep from continually asking myself, *What have I tried? What's going on? What's the vision?* For changes of scenery, we'd go out to the patio, walk around the lake, or sit and stare at the water. There weren't many restaurants around, and when we finally found one, they gave us a tiny salad that was about the size of Will's fist.

We focused on what I wanted to accomplish and who I wanted to help. He started to take me through his process, which he calls the Breakthrough Method, which entailed walking back through my entire journey. We took out a sheet of paper, and he had me write all the most impactful experiences I've had in my life, good and bad, all the way up to the present. After that, we looked for the wisdom I gained from each one. Some of the parts really struck a nerve in terms of how they made me feel, and each experience taught me something.

He told me there's a powerful lesson in each of these experiences. You didn't go through this because you're a victim or because you were born to suffer. When you find out what these lessons are and learn from them, it will change your life—and then you will help change the lives of others.

Things started to click. Considering how I could share my wisdom in a way that served others was where the real magic and insight came from. It took a couple of hours, but when it started to hit, everything changed. The whole time I'd been thinking like a victim, and that I wasn't good enough because I didn't have a college degree. Having a college degree was actually the best thing to happen for me. Without going through what I went through, I would not have been able to achieve the level of success that I did. It was a massive reframe.

And when I tell you that going through this process was emotional? I was in that bad boy crying! "I'm not good! I fail at everything that I do!"

Gradually, everything started to make sense, and in a way that even transcended business. I realized so powerfully that I'd gone through all my personal trials for a reason. I realized that I could distill everything I've learned and use it to help others. *That* was the breakthrough effect. The process helped me unload so much of the baggage that I had been carrying around *and* use it to help other people avoid the same heartache. Even the core of this book came out of that day. I originally wanted to call it *Defying Gravity*.

As I was going through the exercise and writing everything out, one thing really stuck out: that first interview at American Airlines where I didn't get hired. Years later, it *still* got to me. I had the CISSP. I had the experience. And they *still* didn't hire me.

My brother could see how passionate I was about that. "That's it! Right there. You went and you got all these certifications that they said you needed. They told you that you'd be able to pick your salary and work wherever you wanted to work. *All* you needed was that CISSP. You went for it so hard that it *ruined your marriage*. Then, when you got it, did any of that happen? Nope. How did that make you feel? And how many IT people out there are probably dealing with the same thing?"

That really got me thinking. It sunk in at a deeper level how much chasing those certifications cost me and how it didn't pay off nearly how I thought it would. In the interim, every time somebody asked me for career advice, they would always ask what certifications to get. Then I thought back to later, when I was finally working for American Airlines and I met those three business analysts who were working on a security team with me. They had no IT background or cybersecurity experience but were making great money and crushing it, all because they knew this one core security framework.

I put two and two together, and it became the basis of a completely different type of marketing strategy. I went online and spent an entire day researching marketing: how to attract people, what makes people click links, what makes people buy, what to say to get your target audience to listen. I had a new idea, and I always knew who I was targeting, but now I really *felt* my audience's pain point, because I went through it so painfully myself.

Once I started translating my insight into something I could use, Will was telling me, "Write that shit down!" Once I did, we had to go shoot that video *immediately*. I put on a nicer shirt and a blazer—I always have them hanging in my back seat, just in case—and we went down into the lobby and just started shooting. There were still random people walking around, and I could have cared less. Writing everything down was ultimately just practice. I was so inspired that everything rolled off the top of my head:

Remember how you felt when you finally got the certification that you'd been studying for *for months*? Day and night.

You finally got it. I know exactly what you mean. For me, it was the CISSP certification. I studied for *so long* for that certification, and I finally got it. I was excited.

Why? Because they told me this thing was going to give me access to a six-figure income. I'd be able to pick where I wanted to work. So I acted on that belief. In fact, I went and interviewed at the largest airline in the world, American Airlines.

I went through the interview, and the interview went well—until the very end, when they told me that I didn't have the skills that they were looking for. I was confused. I'm like, wait, wait, wait. I got the CISSP, I made everything on the job description, but I'm missing something?

So I went back to the drawing board, and I discovered something that was hidden in plain sight. It was right there the whole time. The one skill that separates IT guys from those that have authority, can choose where they want to work, and how much income they want to earn.

Fast-forward two years later. I went back to American Airlines, but this time I went back with confidence and authority. I interviewed, and I landed the job, but this time as the senior security architect for the entire organization. The guy that didn't hire me—well, he had to report to *me*, because I was running everything.

Listen: this is what I want to teach you. I've been able to transform the lives of so many IT professionals, teaching them this one skill that completely transforms their life without these certifications. I'm looking for bright, ambitious IT guys that want to accelerate their careers, that want the income. They want the authority and the respect that they deserve.

If that sounds like you, I want to invite you for an opportunity to apply for my program. It's by application only, because I only want to work with the best. Click the button below, fill out the application, and we'll set up a call.

If this new opportunity is right for you, we'll invite you into the program so that you can join the other IT guys, right now, that are experiencing the power and authority of having these new skills that have completely transformed their lives. I'm looking forward to talking to you. You just gotta hurry up, because we only have a limited amount of spots in this program. Click the button below to apply, and I'll talk to you soon.

As soon as we posted the video, a comment came through from a guy named Junior. Will told me to message him *immediately*, and when I did, he told me about what he was trying to do, and his challenges in doing it. Will was all excited, telling me to get him on the phone—we both knew that if I got someone on the phone, I could sell.

"Hey, I'd love to talk to you about this. Let's get together tomorrow."

I sent him the calendar link, he filled out the application, and we talked. He was so excited, but he couldn't afford the program—at that time, it cost $2,800. He ultimately called his grandma, and she loaned him the money to enroll—the day after we posted the video. In the end, he went and started his own IT business.

There's a direct correlation between the value you bring and the paychecks you receive. Most people make the mistake of complaining when problems arise. Change your perspective and think like a consultant—a good consultant will see a problem and immediately see an income-producing opportunity. Write out five of the biggest challenges you've seen in your company or industry, then brainstorm a solution for each problem. Can your solutions be turned into business opportunities?

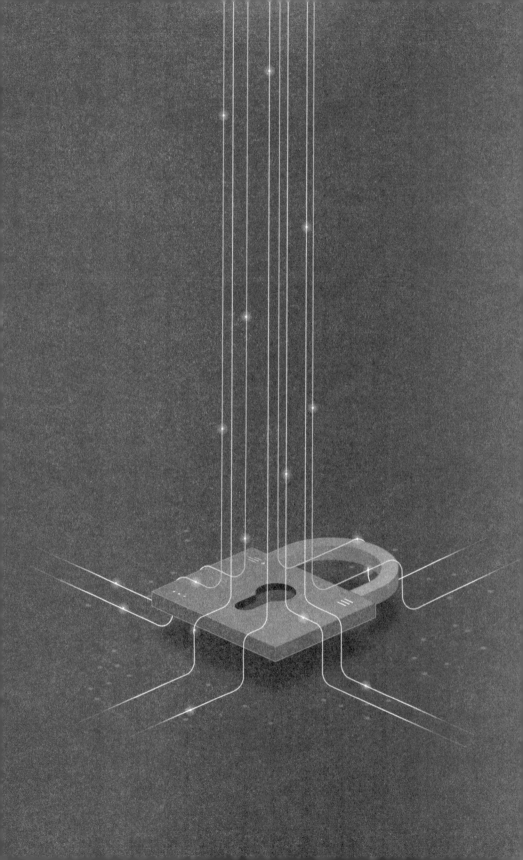

CHAPTER 8

Baxter Clewis II—Blowing Up

It was on from there. The video blew up and filled our first class. I ran it continually for nine months, and that ultimately netted me around two million. After a few weeks, things just took off. After seeing what his process did for me, Will really saw there was something to it. I was the first person he took through it, and by now hundreds have followed. Will's Breakthrough Method is still the first thing my students go through. It's that important.

Before my brother figured it out, I didn't understand anything about digital marketing. I learned everything about that from him too. He played a huge role in the beginning, helping us formulate our sales process, and in developing the Authority Mindset. We spent hours in the office together coming up with that name. I was calling him all the time about strategy. His advice helped us earn the first fifteen or twenty thousand, and we invested that right back into our initial growth. When we kicked off the first class, he did it with me live. He still works with our sales team monthly, and with our students quarterly—always focusing on mindset.

The first thing I learned about marketing once I succeeded was to get the right message in front of the right audience. I started with the right audience, but my initial *message* wasn't resonating. To put it another way: don't try to sell sausage pizza to vegans. I had started out selling a dream, but my audience wasn't at the point where they could even remotely identify with the dream I was selling.

I had to shift my focus to my audience's—and my own—pain point. One I made that shift, the feedback was instantaneous. Over and over, people said, "That's exactly what I experienced. I'm tired of all these certifications. They haven't helped me." Once I understood that, it was easy to come up with a marketing strategy.

Today, my understanding of marketing is ever evolving. If you want to have a successful business, you need to *continuously* study marketing. On top of sending the right message to the right people, you need to spend money to get your message out. I didn't have a big following on Facebook, Instagram, or LinkedIn, and my Facebook friends weren't IT people.

I had to take it upon myself to figure out how paid advertising with Facebook and Instagram worked. I downloaded an online course, and pretty soon, everything clicked.[3] Once I got the hang of it, I was able to reach a *huge* quantity of people. At that point, you're playing a numbers game. Once I targeted my audience, 20–30 percent of the people who saw my ads ended up filling out my application.

When my second cohort got results, they sent in video testimonials, and I created marketing campaigns around those. Advertising their results filled up the next group. We raised the cost of the program to $7,000. Seven students signed up, and of those, five landed great jobs.

---

3   Joel Erway, Programs, accessed January 30, 2023, https://www.joelerway.com/programs/.

BAXTER CLEWIS II—BLOWING UP

People were saying that I was relatable and they *wanted to be like me*. Things came back around to my earlier approach: selling a dream. I went back to showing people what that really looks like. I generally travel first class, drive fancy cars, and all that. I started document-ing it all to show my students how *they* could live when they learn the right skills. The point wasn't just to show off—the idea is that anyone with the commitment can do it. I'm not some off-the-charts genius. I'm just leveraging this security framework and adding value to companies.

I was still going deeper and deeper into marketing to figure out how to help more people. Our number-one roadblock was that most of our prospective students simply couldn't afford the program. I formed a partnership with a financing company so we could offer funding for every student. They give a student a loan, and we got paid in full. Of course, this was great for cash flow. Revenue went through the roof.

I was overwhelmed by all the leads. My students don't just go to a website and click a button to enroll for $7,000. There needs to be a consultation where we filter applicants, answer their questions, and sell them on the program. I was initially taking all those calls, and I quickly got overwhelmed. I still had a full-time job!

Again, I had to get creative. I pulled in some guys from the Philip-pines, taught them how to sell high-ticket products, and put them on the job remotely. I still didn't have a ton of money, and the labor was inexpensive. They ultimately did pretty well—we were consistently bringing in between $30,000–$40,000 a month. It happened so fast.

Now that I didn't have to take all those calls, I shifted my focus to handling demand. I needed someone to answer high-level questions and provide guidance so I could focus on higher-level things. I recruited one of my best students for a new position. He always followed all my directions, checked all the boxes, and was consistently asking me great questions. I knew he'd be good. When I asked him if he'd like to work for me, he couldn't believe it.

Next, I had a conversation with my friend Joel. When he asked how business was going, I told him about my salesmen in the Philippines and how they were doing. He asked what their conversion rate was, and I didn't know. Shame on me—again, you don't know what you don't know. I just knew we were making money. After some digging, I found out that my guys were converting at 10 percent. Joel informed me that a decent closer should be converting around 20 percent and that superstars can do up to 40 percent.

He recommended that I talk to his friend Cole, whose company hires, trains, and recruits salespeople, then uses them to help business owners scale their companies. I was a little nervous about all this. My brother had warned me: once you start working in digital marketing, everybody knows somebody that's selling something to help you. But I trusted Joel. I wanted to at least have a conversation with Cole's people and see what they could do.

I went in and told them we were doing $40,000 a month, and that my guys were converting at 10 percent. They walked me through their process and offered to train and send me two A-1 American closers. When they asked what my goals were, I even amazed myself when I told them I wanted to make $100,000 a month. At this, Cole was just like, "Okay, cool." I couldn't believe it. He told me, "It's no big deal. We have people in our program that are doing a million-plus a month." All this was unimaginable to me.

I signed up, hired their two salespeople, and took them through our training process. The impact was immediate. As advertised, they consistently closed at 20 percent. We went from seven or eight students a month to twenty or thirty. I had to let my guys in the

Philippines go. Within a month, we hit $100,000. The next month, I quit my consulting job.

I was still massively overwhelmed. My social media advertisements started to get a hundred comments in a single day, on top of a hundred or so private messages on average. It all gave me anxiety. Some of these comments and messages would inevitably be from trolls. People would call me a scam artist. "He's just going to take your money." "There's no way he can help you get a job." "You need fifteen years of experience and a college degree."

I'm extremely sensitive about my stuff and am quick to go off on a troll. I just don't have the emotional intelligence to respond gracefully. Tiana was like, "You can't clap back at people like that, dude! It looks bad!" She convinced me to hire an assistant, mostly to handle social media. Now I'm not allowed to even *look* at it.

The trolls' comments triggered that old impostor syndrome. I was questioning whether I actually *was* scamming people. After all, not everyone who goes through my program gets a job at the end. But I'm also not *claiming* that everyone does. The next issue was: *Are my prices too high?*

When I discussed all this with my brother, he told me these things wouldn't bother me unless I felt like there was some truth to them. I had to think about that for a minute. "Nah, I know I'm not scamming people. I *do* feel bad whenever people pay me and they don't get results. But those people don't get results when they don't do the work. If they just follow the process, it *works*. I can't shoulder all the responsibility for somebody else's results, but I *can* be there to support them when they actually *do the work*."

As I was wasting time questioning myself, I could feel it killing my creativity. Most people don't realize that whatever's going on inside of your head is going to affect everything that you do. Whether from a business or personal standpoint, mindset is so, so critical. I swore off social media because I can't let that negativity enter my mind. I can't let it drown out my own voice or the voices of the positive people speaking in my life.

Negativity is the killer of progress and dreams. Most people don't have the mental fortitude to get past other people's beliefs, because most people are naturally people pleasers. Often, when people see that others don't support or believe in them, they'll give up before they even start.

Now, as I don't even look at social media, people will come into the program like, "Man, it's finally nice to see you on the Zoom after that great conversation we had on Facebook." I have to be like, "Let me be honest—that was either Tiana or my assistant." I have to explain that they're partly there to diplomatically set the trolls straight. Now my assistant has been promoted, and we have someone else who deals *solely* with social media.

The bigger you are, the bigger a target you become. I didn't know how much internet hate there was. People just seem to hate success.

Some of these people can get crazy. You know you've made it when people start writing fictitious Reddit threads about you. I've had people make up stories; then my real students come in to light the trolls up; then the whole thing gets flagged and taken down. The bigger you are, the bigger a target you become. I didn't know how much internet hate there was. People just seem to hate success.

Despite the trolls, the success kept coming. *Forbes* reached out and published an article. Then *Black Enterprise* did the same. TV interviews followed. We just keep growing and growing. I created a success coach position within the organization, so each of our students has easy access to someone high level and don't have to wait on me. Our success coach is a little like having a guidance counselor at school. He makes sure students are hitting their weekly milestones, because we don't want anybody to come into the program and not get results. He also prays for the students. We pray a lot around here, because this is a God-led company. It was meant to be. There's no way that you start a business in a pandemic and make millions of dollars without God touching it.

We also have a mindset trainer. The Authority Mindset carried me through impostor syndrome, handling tricky situations with executives from huge companies, and all the rest, and now it's helping our students through the program and into their careers. We take the students through exercises to previsualize what they're going to do with their money when they finally make it. It's just like me tacking up that Chrysler Sebring in my office at AT&T.

What we're doing is so unique. There aren't any other programs like ours. I don't really have competition, because the "competition" is still about chasing certifications. Our competitors' programs couldn't care less about their students' mindsets. In most of them, you're lucky if they even pay attention to whether or not you finish. A lot are teaching straight from some book.

We also make sure our students are truly prepared to do the job, and then we support them when they get it. Most people took high school Spanish because they had to. But when they complete their first class, how many people can actually *speak* Spanish? It's the same thing in the IT industry—people get training and pass a test, but they can't actually do the job because they didn't deeply learn anything. We do reinforcement learning, so when our students learn the payment security standard with us, they're fluent in it when they leave. Then they get into interviews and end up knowing more than the people who ultimately give them the job.

Having an Authority Mindset means not looking at your job as a simple employee-employer relationship. It's about managing your career like it's a business. It makes you focus on continually solving problems and adding value. When you apply that thought process to your career, it changes how you approach everything, and that changes your income.

In turn, businesses do not grow without sales and marketing, and most IT people don't grow their careers simply because they don't market or sell themselves. If you don't market, nobody out there will know what it is you can do. Most people, and especially most IT people, don't brand themselves. The reason I've been able to secure a $200,000 job without even submitting an application was because I marketed and branded myself as *the* guy for PCI. In simple terms, I let people know what I could do.

When our students bring this value and understand that they are marketing and providing a specialized service, they can command the pay that they desire. And crucially, they don't work for anything less than what they desire. Our students do not settle. If a company's not willing to pay their desired rate, number one, we're never going to waste time on an interview. We're going to ask what the client's budget for a given position is *beforehand*. If it's not enough, then all we say is, "Thank you, and I appreciate the opportunity, but that's not what I'm looking for right now."

We don't waste our time or anyone else's. We are specialists. We understand our value. As a result, we're not going to get lowballed.

We're not IT people—we're business technology professionals, and we understand that the value we bring saves the companies we work for money from fines, penalties, and loss of reputation.

The average IT worker rarely understands why he or she does anything. If you ask an IT person, "Hey, why are you installing those patches on the system?" they're going to say, "Number one, it's 'patch Tuesday.' Number two, it's one of my job responsibilities. Number three, I was told to do it." *Classic* IT talk. These people wonder why they're not getting paid, and it's because they don't understand the business side of the equation.

A business technology professional with an Authority Mindset understands that they're removing vulnerabilities from critical systems to protect reputations, avoid fines and penalties, and maintain GDPR, Sox, and PCI DSS compliance. If a company fails to do this, there can be huge implications. *This* is why we're installing patches.

The name of the game is to add value because *people are compensated for the value that they bring*. Most people never achieve the income they want because they simply don't bring value. The question you have to ask yourself is, "If I didn't do my job today, how would this company be affected?" If the answer to that question is, "Not at all," and you're not making a lot of money, don't be surprised.

If my position had been eliminated at the companies I was working for or if I didn't show up, all hell would've broken loose. That company's not going to be compliant, they're not going to know how to run their security program, and they're going to lose millions of dollars in penalties. So you better *believe* they paid me well. If I had stuck around cutting sandwiches or fixing computers, no one would have missed me all that much.

What's the big picture? *That* is what we teach, and *that* is why our students are successful. We teach them how to think. If I want to learn something, I have to give of myself and put in the time to learn a craft. That craft will produce fruit in my life when I share it with others. By adding value and being of service, I'm going to produce a harvest. That's what it all comes down to.

Get a mentor—now! Whenever you set your intentions on doing something great, whether it be starting a business or making a career transition, you'll need a support system. Think about the bold, audacious goals you've created for yourself. Search your network to see if anyone has accomplished what you want to achieve, and see if you can work on getting them in your corner for when you need to navigate challenging circumstances.

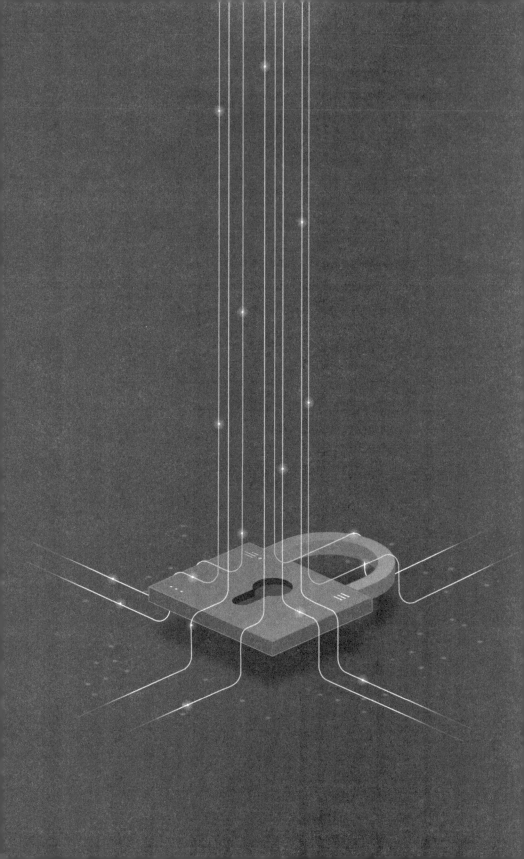

CHAPTER 9

Baxter Clewis III—Impact

I've learned and invested lot to get here, and this is just the beginning. There are still fewer than twenty thousand people on the face of the earth that are certified in PCI, and most of them have no idea what they're doing. On top of this, at the time of writing, there are twenty thousand open positions on LinkedIn for this skill set, and when you look at open positions related to broader certifications, there are *millions*. We're just so niche. Employers come to me every week looking for graduates. I had ten alumni last year making over $200,000. People quadruple their income in months. Our program is six months, but many of our students land a new job within ninety days.

Our current enrollment is over five hundred, with another seven hundred in the self-study course. To date, we've helped over four hundred people land jobs. I get news of my students getting great jobs nearly every day. People are even taking the independent self-study course *on their own* and getting jobs. Hundreds of people are transforming their lives. That's the most rewarding part of all.

My main focus now is helping my students and encouraging other minorities to look at careers in cybersecurity. Number one, they're high-paying careers. Number two, they're not going anywhere. Three, 99 percent of my students are black, and we're significantly underrepresented in tech. Being part of that change fires me up.

One of my first students, Matthew, came to me laid off, unemployed, and broke. He'd been a schoolteacher and wanted to do better for his family. I saw something in him, and I knew I could help. I told him: *If you join me, I will walk you through this process. I will take your career to the next level.* To this he said, "I'm gonna trust you, man. I saw that you're a minister, so I'm gonna trust you. I'm gonna give you everything I have."

He paid for the program by putting it on two credit cards. He gave me his last, and he did great. Every time something came up, he did exactly what I told him to do. The ones that *aren't* successful passively watch our videos and think things are just going to click. Some students just run through our training modules, tell us they "finished the training" within a month and that they don't feel like they know what's going on. These kinds of people think I'm going to land the job *for* them.

Matthew was the opposite. Six months into the program, he secured an interview for one of the largest financial institutions in the world, nailed it, and landed the job. They brought him on as a risk management analyst for a salary of $84,000, the most he'd ever made. He went from unemployed to making $84,000 in six months. When he started, cybersecurity was all new territory for him. I helped him get his bearings, just like Jay did for me at American Airlines. Within ninety days, he was promoted and hired as full-time employee. Nine months in, his salary was raised to $117,000, with benefits, working remotely. Now he's killing it and leading his own assessments.

I still wish he could see himself more the way his clients see him: very, very sharp. He came in hungry, and the people that get the best results are like him: they're hungry and understand their why. In other words, *Why am I doing this?* For Matthew, his relationship with his spouse and his children was rocky because he hadn't been able to provide financial security for them. Once he had stable employment, his relationship with his family blossomed. It's about so much more than money—money's just a vehicle.

We're transforming lives *within* the company too. A great example is one of my best friends, Tim. He hit me up during a tough time, after a terrible car accident. I told him, "Man, I'm not going to give you any money, because that's not going to help you. But I *will* teach you how to *make* money."

I'll always consider a person's skills first. I wouldn't have just hired him because he's my friend. Tim's a great connector. The guy has never met a stranger. He can talk to and connect with anyone, and I need those type of people on my team as enrollment advisors. I knew it'd be a great move for him. If he had another skill set, I would've encouraged him to do something else.

After watching our testimonials, he was thinking, *Man, I want to be a part of this*. After I taught him our process, he came in and immediately started connecting with prospective students. They're getting great results and even thanking him for enrolling them. I had to tell him: you must be on the right track when people spend $15,000 and thank *you* for taking *their* money. He went from making $35,000 a year at his job in LA to making over $10,000 a month working with us. By helping our students change their lives, his own life completely changed.

Cynthia, another one of our friends from church, randomly told us that she had lost her job and was looking for something new, so we told her to send us her résumé. We had a vague idea of her background from a career standpoint, but it hadn't been at the front of our minds. When we looked it over, it was immediately clear that she'd be a perfect fit for the company. We needed a new administrative assistant at that very moment. She was blessed in quickly being able to replace the job that she'd just lost, and *our* company was blessed because she's dope.

When you're trying to find where to go next, don't just look at what's on your résumé. What do other people appreciate about you? Brandon, who's by far our most popular success coach, just loves ministry. He just naturally pours into people and thrives in a space where he can pray for you, prophesy over you, encourage you, and push you. It has nothing to do with any of his background—it's just an innate part of his personality. And through us, he found a job that he absolutely loves doing. Everyone has always talked about the fact that Brandon is an encourager and the ultimate hype man, and those qualities serve him well in his role.

We have multiple people on our team who didn't fully anticipate how their past work would translate into what they're doing now.

Sometimes people get so trapped in the work they've always done that it's hard to see outside it.

Sometimes people get so trapped in the work they've always done that it's hard to see outside it. Looking into a totally different industry can completely transform your financial situation. Another employee, Stephen, used to work in a psych ward where his personal safety was being threatened on a regular basis. Now he doesn't have to deal with that but is still helping people transform, push through personal crises, overcome mindset issues and emotional barriers, *and* tangibly change their lives—while making 30 percent more.

We also brought on Courtney, a former teacher and one of my high school friends, and quickly promoted her to manager. Now she's in charge of our success coaches. She gets to do what she loves— teaching and leading—but doubled her income, got out of a miserable situation, and doesn't have to deal with the bureaucracy of teaching. Courtney was always good with helping students navigate and learn. Now her students are just a bit older. She's phenomenal as a success coach because at the root level it's what she's always done and loves doing.

I used to get asked about my weaknesses in job interviews. My answer was always the same: I expect everybody to bring my same energy in the pursuit of excellence at work and don't have a lot of patience for people who don't. Some people understood that, and others would give me blank stares. I'm just the kind of guy that gets things done, and I've worked with a lot of people who don't. After all, that's how I'm in the position I'm in now: if that guy hadn't been falling asleep on the job, everything would have turned out differently.

Leadership sets the tone for *everything*. For my company to grow, I need to lead it. It doesn't just happen. When I first started the company, I had to do everything. Relinquishing control to focus on high-level things has been a game changer. I don't manage my sales team anymore. I promoted my top sales guy to manager, and we continue to climb because I've set a standard of leadership and accountability that courses down though him and the entire organization.

I can't say it was easy. Sales is *the* most important part of a business. It's the heart of your cash flow. I wouldn't go so far as to call myself a control freak, but giving up control there was hard. Even bringing on an assistant was hard—it was an adjustment to stop checking my own email. Because I'm not a micromanager, I struggled with trusting that people would consistently follow through. I'd just rather just do the job myself than micromanage—I'll fire someone before I have to micromanage them. I've had to let several people go simply because they weren't meeting their marks.

I also had to learn how to build out standard operating procedures to measure and track as much as possible. Not doing that is a large part of why I wasn't as successful in business early on. I was making decisions primarily on emotion. Now I have very specific targets throughout the business, so when something isn't lining up in the numbers, I know *exactly* what to focus on. This is one of the reasons why the company is growing so quickly. We have really good numbers and margins because I'm dialed in to what's important and not getting distracted by the small things.

I've also learned that it's hard to do business on your own. I can't talk million-dollar problems with people who have never made six figures. Everyone under me can come to me with questions, but as a CEO, you have no one above you to go to for clarity. For a long time, I didn't know who I could talk to about all this besides Tiana.

I've learned to take a community approach. Here I have to give another shout out to Cole Gordon. I don't know where I'd be without his group, Eight-Figure Boardroom. We get together quarterly for mastermind meetings, and people come in and talk about different elements of business: tax finance, scaling, marketing strategies, how to do less and get more done efficiently. Just being around these types of people has been phenomenal for my success. If I didn't have these guys from Cole's group in my corner, I don't know where I'd be.

I talk with Cole and my business advisor, Dave, just about every day. When something comes up and I need guidance, we set up meetings, and they give me strategic advice on how to lead. Dave is the ultimate support guy. He manages sales accounts and has really helped me break out of my shell. He reviewed my sales calls when I was still making them, refined our processes, helped me hire new salespeople, prepare for the challenges ahead, set goals, and more.

In March, when I first came on, the goal was to be making $100K a month. To this he'd say things like, "Okay: Here's where you are now, and here's what's going to happen next. Now that you have more traffic coming in, you're going to run into fulfillment issues. Have you thought about getting an admin? Have you thought about bringing on success coaches?" My transition has been so much smoother with these kinds of guys in my corner. Had I done it on my own, it would've been horrific.

We still have ups and downs. I recently had to fire two people because they weren't performing, and having to do that put me in a bad mood for most of the week. Then, suddenly, it all just left me, and I walked into the office with a big smile on my face. The receptionists were looking at me like, *What's gotten into him?* I just had to refocus on how happy I am to be here. I realized that I was mostly mad because we've only made $800,000 this month when our goal was a million. I was talking to my mom and told her if my biggest problem is being mad that I only made $800,000 this month, life is good.

Creating a business or career path that transforms lives is worth more than gold. Tiana and I have used our company and financial resources to help countless people, and our generosity was planned before our success ever happened. What's your plan after you become successful? I want you to write down three ways you'll positively affect the people around you after you've accomplished your big goals.

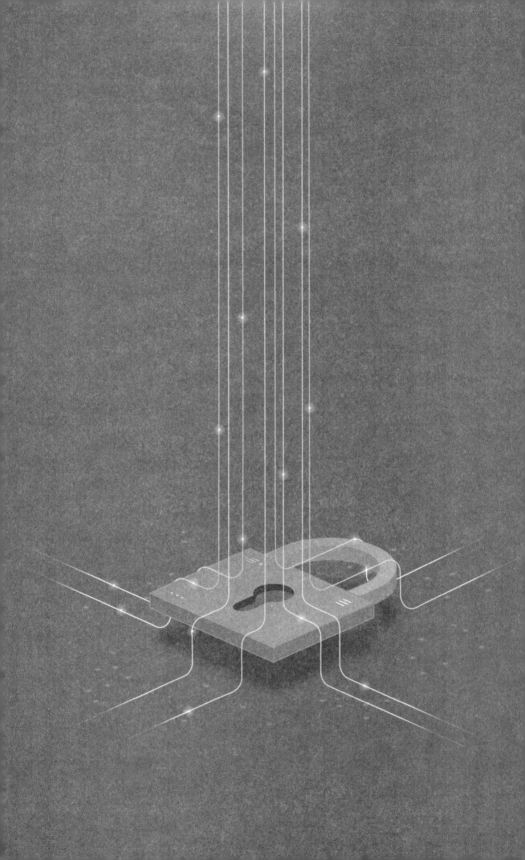

CHAPTER 10

The Mental Health Code

My challenges now are mostly mental. I'm in a place where I under-stand business and marketing and have the financial resources to do other things. But just because I *can* doesn't mean that I *should*. For example, I was going to start a staffing company to place our students, but that entails all the stress that comes along with starting a new business. Financially, we're doing well. My students are getting results. My employers are happy. Tiana and I are debt-free. We paid off all our student loans, cars, and everything else. I'm just so thankful to be in this position. Why would I put additional stress on myself and my family and mess this all up just to make more money?

Now I spend the first three hours of the day on personal devel-opment. I hit the gym, listen to audiobooks, meditate, and drop the kids off at school. I start my workday at 10:00 a.m., do everything I need to do, pick up my kids from school at four o'clock, and then I'm done. I leave work at work.

I still get crazy ideas and am still tempted to jump on them right away, but now I just write them in my journal and keep them in the backlog. I'm not a guy that obsesses about money. Spending time with my kids is what's most important to me. I don't know when I'm going to die. I don't want them to be the kinds of kids that say, "My dad bought me everything I wanted, but he never spent any time with me." I want to make sure they get all the experiences and quality time they deserve.

It took years of focusing on self-mastery to begin to understand all this, and I learned a lot of that came through therapy. It taught me that I am not my feelings. Being afraid or nervous during public speaking doesn't make me a scared *person*. Fears are just feelings, and just because you feel something doesn't mean you have to act a certain way. I may wake up sad for some reason, but that doesn't give me permission to be depressed and lay in bed all day. I need to get up and get to the office, because I have things to do. On the other hand, I know I can be manic, but that doesn't mean I can go spend $10,000 on a shopping spree just because it temporarily makes me feel good. This is about actively choosing what will help me accomplish my goals, even though I might not feel a certain way out of the gate.

I had to fire my first therapist. I initially just went with the first one my insurance provider recommended. My only real criterion was to be able to see someone in person instead of remotely. Then I called him when I was having a bad manic episode.

"Hey, man, we need to talk."

He was like, "Okay, schedule an appointment."

"No, no. *Now*, man. I really need to talk to someone *right now*."

"You have to schedule an appointment."

"Really? I'm telling you I'm having an *emergency* right now, and you're telling me to schedule an appointment? If you're answering the phone, clearly you can talk!"

That was the end of that relationship.

After that, I went back online, read reviews, and *did the research.* My new therapist, Dr. Jay, has a daughter who is bipolar, so she intimately knows what I'm going through. Again, the big lesson is that *you don't have to act out of your feelings.* It's like watching a sad scene in a movie: it might evoke certain emotions, and you might even shed a tear if it's done really well, but it doesn't necessarily make you *sad.* You're not *depressed* when the movie's over, and

The big lesson is that *you don't have to act out of your feelings.*

you don't have to go and act down all day just because you saw some sad scene in a movie.

Despite everything, dealing with bipolar is still a major everyday struggle. The last time I had a manic episode, I got so mad that I threw a lamp through the wall, snatched Tiana's glasses off her face and snapped them in half, kicked in a car door, and generally went berserk, all because I didn't like the way she responded to me about something. This is why staying on my mental health routine and taking my medicine every day is nonnegotiable.

The lows of bipolar start first thing in the morning. Sometimes it's a struggle just to get out of bed. If it wasn't for having to take my kids to school in the morning, some days I wouldn't even *get* out of bed. The lows and the highs can be so extreme. Once those thoughts get into your mind, it can feel like there's no reason for living, even when you know they're not real. I actively deal with this every day.

But now, even when I'm extremely agitated, I don't snap. Normally I end up just running my hands under cold water to calm down, remove myself from the situation, and do breathing exercises. Above all, I don't put myself in high-stress situations if I can help it. I try to live as stress-free as possible—not only for my sake but for my family's. Nobody likes stressed-out Boyd.

People don't quite understand the effort it takes just to put myself in a room and smile sometimes. Coming from a low moment to show up to teach four or five hundred people who paid you to inspire and teach them—I really have to put on that alter ego sometimes. It takes everything in me to pull myself out. Then, when the moment's over, I crash.

It initially surprised me to be a pretty happy guy who was ultimately dealing with depression. At first I didn't know how to deal. Why do I feel sad when I have no reason to? It's totally illogical: my family is healthy, debt-free, financially solid, and we're having a great run in business. Despite all that, sometimes my mood can just get low to the point where, despite everything, you find no enjoyment in life. It doesn't matter what you do; there's just no joy. It's a horrible, hopeless feeling, and I hate it. I'll take the manic highs that come with bipolar all day. My *wife* probably wouldn't, because it can make me super-crabby. But the worst of it comes from the depressive lows, when you don't want to talk to anybody or do anything.

It's strange, but I don't remember much of the lows growing up. I remember more of the highs, and how that made me act out. The lows came later in life. Some people think that money is going to make them happy and solve all their problems, then they ask how people like Robin Williams could kill themselves. They just don't understand the power of mental illness. When you're depressed, it's illogical. It doesn't matter what you have going on in life. Whatever story you're telling yourself in your mind—in that moment, it's true. Outside of death, how can you really escape your mind?

But now, at least, my understanding is a lot further along. I can't let myself get to the point where I feel that hopeless and just want to die as a result. It's so important to be here for my kids, because I've seen how suicide can affect a family. My brother-in-law died by suicide in February 2020, and to see what that did to my wife, my mother-in-law, and even to me? My *goodness*. I never want to see my wife, children, friends, or family in anything even close to that type of pain. This is why we keep our support network strong.

I show up to therapy every week. Up or down, rain or shine. It's helped me understand what triggers my bipolar cycles, and that helps me counteract them. One of the things that really used to launch me into a downward spiral was immediately waking up, checking my email, browsing social media, and consequently being under the spell of all the negativity you find in those places. My day ended up controlling me, instead of the other way around.

Now my phone is on do not disturb from ten at night to ten in the morning, and my mornings are dedicated to personal development. I'm working out, hydrating, doing devotionals, reading, and meditating. I started with guided meditations, then gradually took off the training wheels. Some people think meditation is this spiritual thing where you sit cross-legged and make *om* sounds. At its core, meditation is simply focusing your mind on something very specific, and when your mind loses focus, you refocus. It sounds simple, but of course it's difficult.

Some monks can have tea and simply meditate on their tea. The focal point isn't so important. Mine is interesting: I meditate on my wife's legs. Because those legs … I just love 'em. I sit there with my headphones on, playing music, and whenever my mind drifts to something else, I bring it right back to those legs. In the end, it's just about *training the mind*.

In terms of general preparedness, sleep and meditation are *the* main nonnegotiables. I make sure to get *at least* seven hours of sleep at night. It keeps me from going manic, refreshes my mind, and kills decision fatigue. Willpower is finite. I had to set up a routine to have the fortitude to be able to successfully tackle things that I don't like. Being a CEO and a leader, I have to do all kinds of things that I *don't* like to do, and that's always easiest in the morning, when my willpower is at its greatest. When I used to say I'd work out in the evening, I'd always end up making an excuse. When I get after it when I first wake up, I always get it done.

I also always know what I'm going to wear the next day, even for my workout, so it's one less decision that I have to make. Even though he's weird, Mark Zuckerberg is one of the greats. I love that he and Steve Jobs just wore the same thing every day. I myself am way too fashionable for that, so I just make sure to figure everything out the night before.

At this point, I know myself pretty well. My son asks me every morning to take him to the doughnut shop. I tell him, "I'll give you the money, and *you* can go, but *I'm* not going." If I go to that doughnut shop, I'm going to eat a bunch of doughnuts, and I'm trying to stay in shape. I'm going to completely remove the temptation because I know that sweets are my weakness.

Self-discipline and self-mastery are the keys to life. Growing up, I idolized Bruce Lee and Kobe Bryant because they're just the kings of self-mastery and discipline. Most people fail to accomplish their goals because they're not disciplined. On top of that, they set themselves up for failure because they don't understand themselves.

My brother's lesson in self-mastery was teaching me to get to the root cause of why we want or do things. When I was chasing certifications, I was trying to live a life of financial freedom, but I couldn't articulate that at the time. And when you can't articulate something, it's difficult to marshal support from others in what you're doing. I didn't clearly explain my ultimate goal to my ex-wife, so to some extent it just looked like I was doing things to do them—and now we know how that ended.

The human mind is just naturally geared against making decisions. When you're getting ready to buy something expensive, your heart starts racing. Every decision I have to make reduces my mental capacity, so I simply try to limit the decisions I have to make. That's why learning to delegate is so important. My assistant manages my calendar, answers my phones, and checks my email. I don't want to waste mental energy on things that aren't pushing me toward my goal, because I need to be as sharp as possible to lead my company and my family.

Once I get through my morning routine and finally head into the office, I'm in a great place because *I've* controlled how my day starts. It makes managing my psychological cycles so much easier. And when I *do* inevitably go through them, my wife and I have a plan. I overcommunicate. I'll tell my family when I think I'm going into a manic cycle, and then I'll just go away. I'll literally just go and check into a hotel for a day. When I'm in that place, whatever I believe in my mind is the truth, and I'm very easily set off. I have four kids and a very sophisticated wife, so there are plenty of opportunities to be set off.

Like all marriages, ours has never been perfect. There were places where things got a little hairy and/or chaotic. It's important to have boundaries and be able to say, *Not today, Satan!* Overall, we were relentless in pursuing our shared vision of success and what we defined as happiness. Are we involved in our church? Are our kids good? Are we eating? Are we serving other people? Are we able to help other people through what we do? All this is in the interest of keeping my support system strong. They're so important, yet we all know people who burn bridges. No matter where you go on your journey, it's important to build and take care of your relationships with people who can support you.

I don't know how far I would've been able to go as an international speaker without my own support system. When Tiana quit working her full-time job to become a financial coach, that put me in the position to do things like fly off to India for a week for speaking engagements. I couldn't have done that if she was holding down a full-time job. Later, we survived taking care of four kids during a contentious period with my ex-wife because we had the support system of my dad, Tiana's aunt, and many others.

When you're isolated, the only voice you hear is your own. That can lead to dumb mistakes, because you don't know where your blind spots are. And at the very least, you're going to need encouragement and someone to talk to, if only to get things off your chest. Especially if you have kids, you're going to need people around to help.

As much as we all want to be rock star parents, we're all human. Even if you don't have family, that doesn't mean that you can't create an amazing support system. We know many people who built their own communities through church and their friends. Be intentional about building your support system and nurturing it where you can. It will play a key role in your success, like it did for me.

The way you think all comes with your circle. You can only grow as high as the people that surround you. If you have nine broke friends, you're bound to be the tenth. I always tell people who aren't yet at the level that they want: *check your circle*. If nobody in your circle is doing what you desire, you need to change your circle. In other words, if you can't change the *attitudes* of the people around you, then you need to change the people around you.

When you get around people who are doing a lot better than you, they talk differently. And depending on what type of person you are, it's either going to do one or two things: it's either going to motivate you like crazy, or you're going to start hating. When people come around me, they're either leave the interaction inspired or miserable.

But I felt like I was successful *before* we started making the money. I defined what success meant to me, and that was my kids living under one roof and eating, my wife being happy, and all of us going to church together. That alone made me successful. I don't understand when people equate their value with their salary or define their success by how much money they make.

I spent a good deal of time running with the wrong people in and out of my teenage years, especially when I moved back in with my mom. Some of those kids were smoking weed and cigarettes, stealing things, acting out in class, and all the rest. Today, several of those people are dead or in jail.

I've always been a big shoe nerd and used to save up for custom Nike Air Force 1s. I'd bring those to my friend who had a little sewing machine. We'd buy fabric from Gucci and Burberry and sew it onto the shoes, so instead of spending thousands of dollars on these super-high-end brand name shoes, we'd get the work done ourselves for $150. Just a few years after we graduated, that same guy went to rob a putt-putt and ended up shooting the cashier in the back of the head. Now he's in prison for life and potentially looking at the death penalty.

I've always been a bit of a rebel. I didn't like following rules, and that didn't work out too well for me. My mom gave me great advice about living, what I should do in college, and all kinds of other things. I didn't follow her directions, and now I have the scars to prove it. Be wise enough to listen when somebody tells you what it is that you don't know. To put it another way: be smart enough to know what you don't know.

When you're too close to things, there are always things you'll overlook or fail to consider. That's why I always at least consult with Tiana. She just has a different perspective on things. The way my life has gone, I tend to automatically gravitate toward the negative. Thankfully, Tiana tends toward the positive. All the time she's asking, "But have you considered *this*?" Most of the time I'm responding, *Nope, I did not.*

As I got older, I realized that *success leaves bread crumbs*. Follow the advice of people that have been to where you want to go. The most successful people in the world have coaches. Professional athletes have coaches. Why shouldn't you? So many people think they can accomplish the things that they want to completely own their own. The highest-paid, highest-performing individuals in the world all have coaches. Even presidents have consultants and speech writers, but most people still think they can just do everything on their own.

I don't believe that we're meant to do life alone. Whether you get a therapist, a counselor, or a spiritual advisor, you have to have somebody in your corner to be there for you during tough times, because tough times will come. Sometimes they're provoked, and others they're unprovoked. You just have to be prepared to roll with whatever it is. Trying to go it alone is a lot harder than having a support system. It's *everything*.

Tiana herself says she never could have become an entrepreneur if she wasn't around my brother and sister and me, and I wouldn't have survived corporate America without Tiana to help me navigate it. A lot of it was in the little things. She'd help me reword emails. She's not always the most tactful person in the world, but she does know how to expertly execute a good old-fashioned corporate clapback. Our skills were complementary.

Tiana also played a huge part in changing my circle. When we met, she was juggling Toastmaster events, women's conferences, volunteering as a poll worker during elections, working with the American Institution for CPAs, and I can't even keep track of what else. She's always running with high-level, financially savvy people.

When I would attend events with her and suddenly find myself talking to the CEOs and CFOs of large companies, I was feeling like the least-educated, dumbest person in the room. It used to bother the heck out of me. Sometimes I *still* don't feel like I belong in some of the rooms she brings me into. For a long time, I was overly nervous and self-conscious about it, which led to more impostor syndrome. After some time I started to get used to it. Fortunately, I'm a chameleon. The street smarts I had to develop through how I grew up always come in handy, no matter who you're around.

Just knowing to keep smiling really helps me, especially when I'm not 100 percent confident in what I'm doing in a given moment. A smile is so simple, but it gives you this jolt of confidence. That's why *crash and burn with the smile* is so central to my philosophy. It doesn't matter how nervous I am—when you see pictures of me speaking, there's going to be lots of teeth involved. It's helpful at least since I was a teenager. When I transferred to my middle school and this bully kid tried to mess with me, I just smiled and then punched his lights out. I learned that trick from *Three Ninjas*. He never bothered me again.

While I still have a chip on my shoulder about not finishing college, I haven't met too many people that are actually doing what they studied in college anyway. Most of the people I know who spent all this money on their degrees aren't even making enough money to pay their student loans back. What a rip-off! Our society as a whole ought to be ashamed of itself for allowing so many eighteen-year-olds to go into six figures of debt, then making it hard to even get a business loan.

I'd still eventually like to be able to get my degree—and at Howard University, like Tiana—just to be able to say that I *finished*. Finishing things is important to me. I'm simply not a quitter. Life might delay things, but I'm *not* a quitter. In my case, it just didn't work out.

At this point, I'm ultimately confident in my abilities. Mostly, that confidence comes from having a plan. That's where I think a lot of people go wrong. They go into tough situations without a plan, and then that lack of preparedness shows up. I also realized that a lot of what I'm doing isn't really taught in college.

I try to transfer that same sentiment to my students, because many of them have the same doubts that I did. They're still concerned about certifications and meeting the made-up experience qualifications for the jobs they're applying for. I have to tell them: I crushed this position at American Airlines, and I *still* don't qualify based on the original job description. *To this day!*

I'm a firm advocate of faking it till you make it. If you can do it, you can do it. You have to believe in yourself. If I had let fear hold me back, I never would've discovered that I was actually good at public speaking. People avoid doing things because they fear failure. Fear is a killer of dreams, but the thing about fear is that it's not real. If I had given in to fear, I wouldn't be where I am today. I was trying to give away a life-changing program for free, and nobody would take it. I could have leaned into the negative beliefs and quit: *If people won't take it for free, how on earth am I gonna sell it?*

Now, when people expect the worst, it makes me highly upset. This might sound weird, but I actually get very irritated when people ask me "what if" questions—or at least negative "what if" questions.

When I buy my daughter something, she'll say, "What if I wear this and the other girls laugh at me?"

My students will ask, "What if I get in this job interview and they ask me this or that, and I don't handle it well?"

I don't care. Don't "what if" me. Don't just sit there imagining the worst.

I don't allow myself to do that, period. Nobody believed that I would jump 6'6". The school that I went to was so poor that we didn't have high jump equipment, so I couldn't practice during the week. Before the track meet would start, I would show up early to practice the day of, and that was all the time I had. If I'd had the equipment and a coach, who knows how good I could have been? I didn't allow those limiting circumstances to sabotage my goal of jumping 6'6". I just knew that eventually I'd get there.

Instead, I always ask myself what's the *best* that can happen. To me, the worst thing that can happen is somebody simply telling me no, and I'm fine with being told no. I don't know if it's the bipolar in me, but I just focus on the upside. In every situation, there's a good and there's a bad. You have to decide which side you give power to. Money is the perfect example: money is amoral, but it can be perceived as good or bad, depending on who you are and where you're at. Everyone wants it, but as soon as you get it, a lot of people see it as suspect and think you should be giving it away.

Whatever you give your attention to, you feed, and it will magnify in your mind as a result. I just maximize, maximize, maximize, and that's probably why I'm a good salesperson. I just stress the high points like crazy. I cannot stand negativity. I've already dealt with so much of it in my life. "You can't do this. You can't do that." Now my response is: *Don't apply your limitations to me. We're not the same.*

Success can destroy a person or business just as quickly as failure can. Most people don't put a plan in place to manage success, and it can ultimately consume them. I deliberately created a routine and keep people around that help manage my success and mental state. I recommend that you do the same. For instance: Have you created a morning routine? When you can control your day, you can manage your outcomes. Take a few minutes to write out a morning routine aligned with consistently conquering your day.

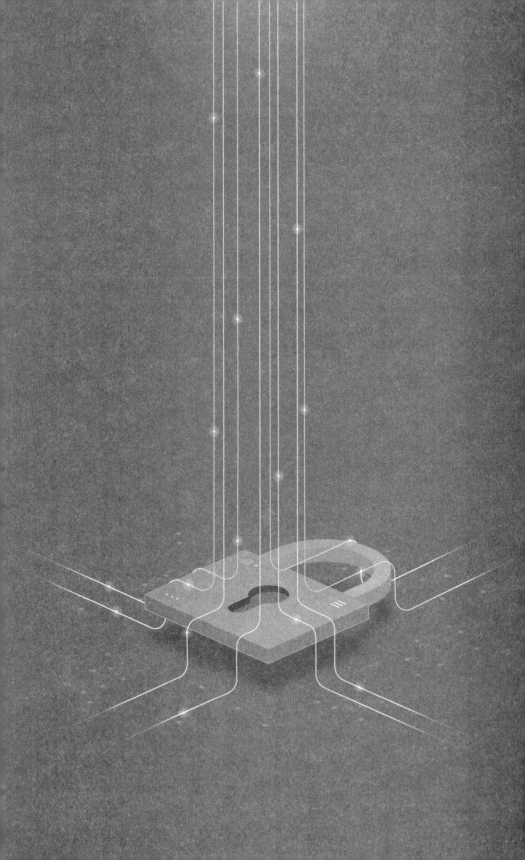

CHAPTER 11

The Calling

I felt the calling to become a preacher in 2013, and I told God no. I dreamed I was in our church, getting introduced by the pastor. "Minister Boyd Clewis is coming to bring the word today." Then I stepped on the stage. Our church isn't that big; it holds three hundred or so people. We have a stage, and two projectors for the people in the back. I saw myself standing up there in a suit. I don't remember saying anything—only being introduced. Then, when I woke up, I was thinking, *Nope! Not happening!* Not *doing it.*

I did go and have a conversation with my pastor about my dream. He was like, "Well, come on then, man! Join the team!" He told me to answer the call and walk through. They do training for ministers at my church, and I was like, *Eh, I don't think so.* I told him I'd think about it, but in my mind I already knew it was a no.

Meanwhile, my sister was saying, "I saw it."

Then my mom said, "Yep. I always knew."

All along I'm like, *Nah, nah, nah.* I wasn't about to go preach. I left that to my dad and my sister and my mom. *Not* for me.

Initially, I was extremely apprehensive about public speaking. I was usually producing things from *behind* the camera. When I was working for the tech team at my church, we did video announcements. One day I ended up filling in when the talent couldn't make it, and my first time on camera was so cringeworthy that I was never invited back. It wasn't so much that I was uncomfortable; it's that I was unskilled.

Despite my phobia of speaking, my family has pictures of me at eight years old, wearing a suit at a microphone, giving a speech at church, smiling, looking so happy. Around that same time, at a revival, one of the ministers put his hand on my head and told me that I would grow up to be a very wealthy man. My sister also has a very strong prophetic gift—she'll tell me things that she saw in her mind; then they end up happening. It's spooky. She told me she saw me speaking on big stages, walking through airports where people knew my name, and that I would be big in the tech industry. Hearing all this for years made me start to live with those beliefs despite the chaos of my youth.

In the end, not listening to God when I was called to preaching was definitely the wrong call. My life went to hell more or less immediately thereafter, and I wholeheartedly believe things went bad because I didn't do what I was supposed to do. My separation and divorce started happening, and I lost interest in everything, including preaching. For at least two months I was in such a dark place that I didn't really leave the house. Hear me now: when God tells you to do something, you should definitely do it.

It wasn't necessarily due to fear or disinterest. My main thought process was, *Who am I to be instructing anyone on their spiritual walk?* I have my own demons to deal with. I've messed up things considerably.

I've sold drugs. I've had kids out of wedlock. I've been arrested. I was just always thinking, *Nah, man. Too much baggage.*

Once I came around and accepted the call, I resolved to just do the work. By that time, I was really succeeding at American Airlines, traveling the world, doing what I love—and with nothing to my name but a high school diploma. I knew I had nobody to thank for all that but God. It was only right that I honor what he was asking me to do, because I knew I didn't deserve any of my good fortune.

The first problem was to figure out what the heck I was going to talk about. Since my dad's a preacher, I went and sat with him. We took a day to just talk about different Bible verses. At church, we usually have a sermon series that revolves around a specific topic, but in my case it was open. For me, the breadth of all possible options complicated things.

So I went back to the Bible. One of my favorite narratives is about a rich leper who was trying to heal himself. Nothing he tried was working, so he took a long trip to see a prophet. The prophet instructed him to dip himself seven times into a dirty river and that it would cleanse him. First off, it took a lot of faith for this rich leper to go see another man about healing. The two of them didn't share a religion, and it was a leap of faith to go and dip himself in this dirty river—not once but seven times. But after he followed the instructions, he came up and "his flesh was restored and became clean like that of a young boy."

I broke that down into a process that other people could use: the story is about having faith, taking action on the word when you receive it, and not giving up. If it doesn't work the first time or the second time or the third time, you need to keep trying. Will you wait seven months? Will you wait seven years? That's the story of my life.

People told me that I would accomplish certain things, but it's not like anyone gave me a timeline.

I love process and formula. I believe that just about anything can be deconstructed and reassembled. I called the first sermon "WFA = M." When you read the titles of my sermons, you won't know what I'm talking about until the punchline at the end. I didn't break it down until the last five minutes of the sermon: word × faith × action = miracle.

My pastor helped me come up with an outline. That really helped, because I don't like to follow scripts. I'm all about bullet points. For weeks I was just recording myself giving that sermon over and over, refining. Finally, the week before, we had our preaching team meeting. I presented the sermon to them for feedback, and they gave me the thumbs up.

The day of was extremely nerve-racking. Normally I get to church at eight thirty in the morning to set up the cameras and equipment. That Sunday I showed up at six thirty. I can still remember unlocking the doors and disarming the security system. I was going over my outline again and again, reciting things in my mind, the whole time thinking, *This is really happening*. I was so nervous my legs were shaking.

My biggest fear was of misleading people ... because at church, people are going to make life decisions based on what you're telling them.

I had spoken in other countries for American by this point, so from a *speaking* standpoint, I was pretty confident. But I would rather speak to ten thousand people about cybersecurity than the three hundred people at my church. My biggest fear was of misleading people. There's a lot of pressure that comes with this, because at church, people are going to make life decisions based on what you're telling them. What you're saying needs to be grounded in truth. The fact that people could make life decisions about their salvation and their souls based on what I said was so much pressure. If I said the wrong thing and misled people, then I'd have to deal with that. It all just made me very, very nervous.

The sermon was about twenty-five minutes long. When I finished, I went back into the greenroom and slumped into a chair. I was so relieved when it was over. Then, almost immediately, there was a knock on the door. "Boyd! There's a whole bunch of people out here who want to talk to you!"

Oh, no. I didn't want to talk to *anybody*. I was beyond tired. I don't think I'd ever been that drained in my life.

Tiana came back there like, "Hey, man, you need to come talk to these people."

"I don't want to. I just talked for thirty minutes. I don't wanna talk to *nobody*."

Most of the congregation didn't know I would be preaching, so it was a surprise for many of them. But my mom knew and invited all her friends. They knew me from when I was a terrible little kid, so they were all in tears: "Oh my God! It's a miracle!"

Once Tiana dragged me out to talk to my family, they all gave me hugs, told me how well I did and how proud they were of me. After I put in some face time with everyone, my mom took me out to lunch, then I went home and crashed for the next eighteen hours.

Now, when we get a raise, Jesus gets a raise. We're not those people who try and hoard and rob from the one who blessed us. Our goal is giving in proportion to our income. We tithe from every paycheck, and we tithe from every profit draw. On top of that, our church does what we call a "resurrection seed." We agreed that the amount we contribute to that has to be extravagant enough *to make us blink*. Next month, we're going to give one of our students $10,000 cash in a referral competition. Of course, we'll make that all back and then some, which will then provide *more* money for us to give.

We have a goal to give away a million dollars in the next year, simply because that money can profoundly change people's lives for the better. Money doesn't have to be a negative thing. I ultimately want to be known as a guy that helped people reach their potential. I hate seeing people trying to accomplish something and stalling because of money—all the more so if their goal is changing lives. I want to see people succeed, start businesses, and generally do fulfilling things out of passion. When you're doing something you're passionate about, it doesn't feel like work. It's all joy.

I know this from personal experience. I've had so many things I've wanted to do that I couldn't afford, and I know how bad it feels to be stuck. Once, when I was married to my first wife, her side of the family was going on vacation, and I simply couldn't afford to go. They were able to take our son along, but they weren't about to be paying for me. My son got to enjoy spending all this quality time with family. Meanwhile, I was back at home, feeling like less of a man because I couldn't afford to take my family on vacation. That really motivated me, because that's definitely not the way I want to live.

Nowadays, we sow where we're led. We donate to all kinds of different causes, whether it's individuals who want to start businesses, charities, or nonprofits. One woman we contribute to works with school districts to create programs for kids who have been suspended. Instead of leaving them to sit around at home, she created an alternative program that proactively helps them correct their behavior and understand its consequences. After being a troubled kid myself, I thought that was very cool. We donated a pretty significant chunk of change to that, because it's obviously something I believe in.

Every time we've been elevated, we've always poured back. We never waited to get to some arbitrary point where we finally had "enough" to give back. Even back at American Airlines, we were still pouring resources back into our church. A lot of the people on my PCI team survived the mass layoffs there during COVID-19 in part because I worked so hard to train and mentor them. Seeing that you could help people not only survive but then *independently* go on to get their own six-figure jobs was one of the main inspirations for starting my training institute.

When we sow, we reap the harvest. Of course, we take care of family first. You have to put on your oxygen mask first before helping others. Once family's taken care of, then we invest in others. I'm paying it forward so everybody can have their own success story. We all need different things. Often, people don't believe that their dreams are achievable until they see somebody that looks like them accomplishing something similar. That's why I'm so hell-bent on sharing my message.

When you're successful and you serve others, you're not just blessing *you*—you bless the world. There's value we're providing through running our business the way we do, and there's value that we're able to provide by pouring ourselves and our resources into other things. There are people at our church who wouldn't be running their businesses if we hadn't been pushing and encouraging them. We have twenty-five employees, and at least ten of them came from our church. We want to increase wealth in the kingdom of God. When the people we're connected to have money and resources, they can give more. When everyone *gives* more, we can *do* more.

If you spend all your time, energy, and effort trying to serve yourself instead of others, you're not going to *experience* success. You may make money, but you're never going to be satisfied. You're never going to find true joy in any of it if you spend all your time, energy, and effort serving yourself.

I had to *start out* serving myself as a teenager to be treated respectfully by my peers, so I went and sold pamphlets for "Reverend" Brown in front of the grocery store. But when I really started moving forward, it was serving others, no matter what was going on. I was trying to buy diapers. I was making sure that the kids were taken care of, and that my stay-at-home-wife was good. I had no choice but to serve others very early on. I ended up acquiring many of the skills I ultimately needed through serving at church. My success grew out of trying to serve others around me.

You have to give to grow. The name of the game is "give, gain, grow." This is all quite biblical: the Bible says that there's seeding time and harvest time. Seeding time actually involves giving and planning, and that in time will grow and deliver fruit. These are universal principles. Jesus came to serve, not to be served. This is really the last and most important lesson: *be not selfish, sucker.*

Instead of providing an exercise for this chapter, I would like to take the opportunity to acknowledge my Lord and Savior, Jesus Christ. I couldn't have accomplished anything without his grace in my life. I'm eternally grateful.

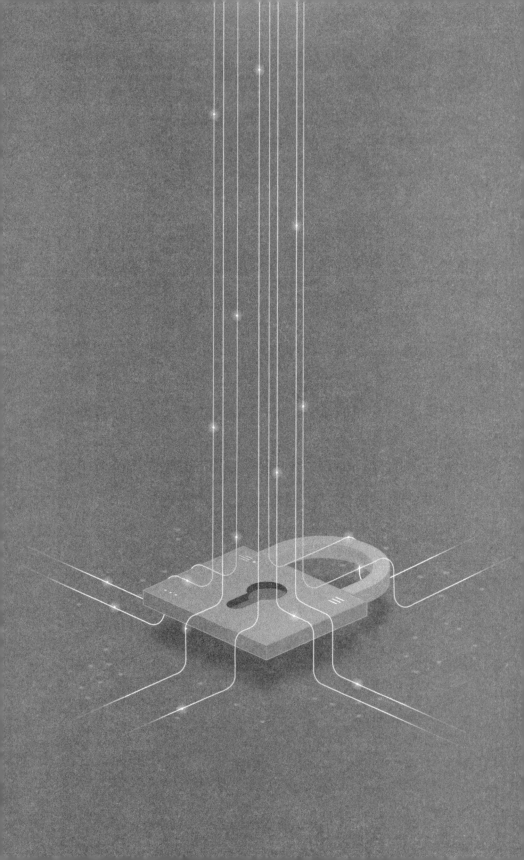

CHAPTER 12

Legacy

Now, legacy is always at the front of my mind. What lasting impression do I want to leave? The values in my household are pretty clear: faith, family, finances. Simple. What are *your* values? What's important to you? If you don't have a map to somewhere, then you'll end up nowhere. And how do you know if you're lost if you don't have a destination? Tiana and I were very clear on what legacy we wanted to leave and what retirement would look like. We're goal-oriented people, and it's hard to leave a legacy when you're not goal oriented.

A huge part of this is considering, *What do I want my kids to remember me by?* I drive my oldest son to school every morning. Before I started my own business, I couldn't do that because I was on someone else's time. Now taking my son to school and picking him up is a joy.

I've just straight-up told him: I don't know how long I'm going to be here. I'm trying to teach you everything that I *didn't* know so that you can be more successful than me. I need you to take these lessons, implement them, live a good life, and teach *your* children in turn. I've been able to accomplish some rare things. If you don't learn this from me, where are you going to learn it from?

Every morning, I try to teach my son some type of lesson about business, relationships, finance, credit, etcetera, then I'll ask him some kind of thought-provoking question about it. According to him, one of the most valuable lessons he learned was something I hadn't realized he really picked up.

> **I've been able to accomplish some rare things. If you don't learn this from me, where are you going to learn it from?**

We were at Walmart one day, and I had parked at the back of the lot outside because I didn't want anybody to hit my car. When we were done, we pushed the cart all the way to the car in the back of the lot, unloaded the groceries, and then I walked the cart all the way back to the return.

When I got back in the car, he asked me, "Why didn't you just leave the cart where we parked, like all the other people around us?"

I said, "Let me tell you something: if you were to ask the people who left these carts all over the place what their income is, I bet it would be extremely low."

He's looking at me like, "Uh, what?"

"How we act in one area of our life impacts every other area. If I'm not going to take the little bit of effort that it takes to return this cart, I'm not going to make the effort it takes to learn a skill, grow a business, or build a career. I'm not the type of person that's going to take shortcuts in any way, whether it's with these shopping carts or with my business."

"That makes sense."

"Now do you see why I'm always on you about picking things up and doing the little things? That's the way things happen. It's also why I encourage you to go hard at practice, because we play how we practice."

Of course, I also put in my time at Sack and Slave. I've been in that position, collecting carts all day, and it's a lot easier to retrieve the carts from their designated stations instead of chasing them all over the lot. I've been there. I'm always telling my team: do the small things. They want all the money, but they don't always want to do all the small administrative things that complete the circle.

Tiana and I are trying to become a wealth incubator in our community so we can also leave a legacy there. Together, we have a bit of a Midas touch: whenever people connect with us, within months, they tend to start making more money than ever before. It just *happens*. Granted, sometimes that's simply because we hire them, and we believe in paying fair wages at our company. It doesn't make sense that pay scales are so lopsided. One of my goals is to make my employees rich and to become richer myself in the process.

We share the philosophy of wealth building and not going into debt, which is yet another huge part of the legacy that I'm trying to leave. I talk to my kids about all this, too, and am extremely transparent with them about our finances. I've explained what it means to go out and take loans to my kids: just because you *have* money doesn't mean that you *spend* the money. I'm trying to impress upon them how to make smart investments, how to choose where to spend money, work ethic, and all these other things I learned the hard way.

Now we're debt-free, but it hasn't always been that way. Last year we paid off around $200,000 to finally clear the slate. That had always been one of our biggest goals. Even when Tiana and I first got married, we were broke. In one of my bipolar hypomanic moments after the divorce proceedings, I had gone on a big spending spree and went through almost all my money.

When I bought the ring, I skipped paying the mortgage on my house. Tiana didn't find out about that until five or six months later. At that point in our marriage, we were trying to find the balance between her semistrictness with money and my own YOLO, spend-it-all tendencies. By the time we'd been married for six months, we had racked up $15,000 in credit card debt. We'd moved to Plano to be closer to my job, and in that process, we'd skipped *another* mortgage payment.

Of course, we didn't want the house to go into foreclosure. Fortunately, we were able to settle all the back pay. Then all the other bills came through. At that point, my salary was sixty-six thousand, and Tiana was making over seventy. Somehow we still ended up in a spot where we didn't have enough money to pay the light bill. In the end, we had to take one of my favorite guns to a pawn shop. Let me put this another way so you hear me right: *our money management was so bad in that first year that we had to sell a gun to keep the lights on.*

Dave Ramsey's Financial Peace University was our biggest step toward becoming financially responsible. It's very popular in churches, including ours. Over seven weeks, there are seven baby steps to take to get out of debt, safeguard the finances of your family, and get to a place where you can start to build wealth. The course taught us the importance of having an emergency fund, both in business and in life. Had we not taken the time, energy, and effort to go through that, we wouldn't be where we are now.

It was huge to create a shared vision, take a journey *together*, and follow a specific road map. It was the first thing in our marriage that made us really start working together as a team. I don't know if or when that would've developed had we kept trying to do everything on our own. We were able to pay off $33,000 in debt in one year *and* buy a new house. Then, after we went through it, we started teaching it in our community.

The big, unexpected lesson from all this was *the importance of actually following the instructions.* So many people seek help, but then they don't follow the instructions. This is something that our unsuccessful students fail to do. They self-sabotage because they think they know better—but if they knew better, they wouldn't need help in the first place. Humans are just naturally going to mess things up. It takes discipline to follow the path of somebody else.

If somebody gives you a proven path to get to a place, it's almost like following GPS. If you follow the route, it's going to get you to the destination. But how many times have we all decided to go somewhere, ignore the GPS because we know the path, and end up in a traffic jam fifteen minutes later? The GPS would have been telling you to take a detour, and instead you're sitting in traffic.

When my brother gave me sales and marketing strategies, I *followed his instructions.* When our partner Cole works with his students, they're constantly bringing me up, calling me "the million-dollar man," because I simply *followed his instructions.* When we were having problems with our payment plans, our coach Dave told us to use Payfunnels and gave us advice on how to structure it. By the time our thirty-minute call was over, we already had Payfunnels set up.

Now that we're debt-free, we're free to pursue the other part of our legacy: generosity. It would be disrespectful for me to be in my position and not give back. I didn't have this sense of possibility when I was younger. I want to be able to reach back and help people in a similar position realize that there's hope for the future. My wife and I are huge givers. Whenever there's a need, whether financial or in general, we're going to be the first ones to help. Of course, we don't believe in financing stupidity, but when there's a real need there, we want to help people succeed. We're extremely generous. We've paid rent for people. We've booked trips for people to take mental vacations. And, of course, we've given a significant amount to the church.

I've bought two cars for people this year alone. Paid in cash. "Here's the keys. Be blessed." One was for a friend from church. He came to me and said, "Boyd, the Lord put it on my heart to start my own trucking business. There's this truck for sale, but I just don't have the money right now. The Lord also put it on my heart to ask you for help, but I had too much pride."

I just looked at him and said, "Done."

"Are you serious?"

"Yep. Done."

He got the truck and started the business.

"I'm going to pay you back."

I said, "No, you're not. You're going to pay it forward."

I don't generally lend, because when I do, I expect it back. When it comes to business and finance, you *will* pay me if you owe me. I don't want to put that kind of strain on my relationships with anybody. So that's why I just don't lend. I gift.

Perhaps most importantly, we're also generous with knowledge. At this point, we understand sales, marketing, finance, and starting and funding businesses. We share those insights with people. We frequently have consultations to challenge people's thinking, because most of them are simply thinking too small. You're not going to become a rich person if you're selling your time for $300. Time is something you never get back. We teach people how to build systems and think like CEOs. You'll reach a point where if you want to grow, you have to start orchestrating and paying people to do things. You have to learn how to take your hands off, just as I did.

Business starts and ends in the mind. If you don't believe that you can do something, you're right, and the results will show it. I was guilty of this same thing myself—early on and even after we started having real success at Baxter Clewis. Our second-year goal was $700,000 in revenue. Then I got around different people—the kind of people who were doing $700,000+ in revenue per month. Their energy transferred, and we ended up doing *three million* that year, which I didn't even think was possible.

Now, in the first quarter of *this* year, we've already done more than three million. We completely blew the previous year's numbers out of the water in ninety days. I'm not sharing this to brag about how much money we have but to show what's possible. We're not celebrities, and we're not famous, but we're still making big moves.

When I see people thinking too small now, I have the experience to see it from a mile away. A girl hit me up on Instagram and said, "Hey, Boyd, I've been following you. I was just wondering if you could give me some advice on how I can take my business to the next level. I have a course, and in the last ninety days, I've made $7,500. But it's not doing as well as I wanted it to."

After engaging her more, it became clear that my brother and I could help her out, so we decided to coach her for six weeks. She was also helping people land jobs in IT, but her focus was on project management. Her students were ultimately getting jobs with salaries of $80,000 to $100,000, yet she was only charging them $1,500. Sound familiar?

I asked her, "Can you help me understand something? How does it make sense that you're helping people make $100,000 a year, yet they only pay you $1,500 for helping them get there in the first place?

A university is going to take at least *eighty grand* from most people, then put them in a position where they're making $40K a year. You're okay with that?"

She was like, "No, but who am I to charge more money?"

I said, "That's your problem right there. You don't see the value in yourself."

From there, we didn't have to change her program at all, but we did change *how she thought about and presented herself.* Then we got her to change her price point. Instead of $1,500, she started charging $7,500. In the subsequent ninety days, she made $89,000.

You're only going to be successful to the extent that you're willing to take a risk. A lot of people tell me point-blank that they want to be in the position that I'm in; then they're ultimately not willing to do what I've done.

I was talking to another guy with an IT course who wrote me, saying, "I want to be just like you, man. I see your ads everywhere and I understand what you're doing, and I want to do the same thing."

I said, "Okay, cool. So I spent at least $40,000 this month on advertising."

And he says, "Aww, no, man. Oh, no. I'm not going to do that."

Well, you're not going to be like me, then!

It's a risk! Sometimes I spend up to $100,000 a month on advertising, because I'm confident that I'll get it back. Most people aren't about to do that, and that's why they're not going to be successful. You can't show me a billionaire or a multimillionaire who's unwilling to make six-figure investments to grow their portfolio. Again, it's a mindset thing. If you don't have that, you're not going to be successful.

It's so important to invest in yourself and seek out people that have been to where you want to go. And you don't have to wait until you're financially successful to do any of this. There's no excuse—

there's someone out there on the internet that's doing well at exactly what you're trying to do, and there are so many free resources.

However, you also have to understand the quality is going to significantly improve when you start *really* investing, simply because you'll have more skin in the game. People that join my program at our higher price point get much better results than the people who bought in at the beginning at $500. If you don't have skin in the game, there's a tendency to be like, *Oh well, I lost five hundred bucks. Big deal.* But at fifteen grand, you're going to be making sure you get your money's worth. It makes you do the work.

I don't understand when people feel like they're "trapped" in a job. You can find a new one! There's an almost sick dependency that some people have in their jobs, and it drives me nuts. Even my mom was that way before she started her real career making money as a teacher coach. She got mad at me when I told her that she needed to quit her job and that she could make more money, especially because she has more degrees than Tiana and I combined.

Her response was, "Well, everybody's not you. We can't all be job hopping to higher-paying jobs. I'm too old for that. People will see that on my résumé, and they're going to say something about it." I was *not* trying to hear that.

There's an opportunity out there that's specifically tailored to *your* experience.

There's an opportunity out there that's specifically tailored to *your* experience. Most people *can* achieve a higher salary. The problem is that they don't believe that they're *worthy* of that salary, and they don't show up with the confidence to command it. If you're not confident that you can do $100,000 worth of work, why would *I* pay you $100,000?

Some people are overly intimidated for no good reason, and it doesn't come out until you really interrogate and examine it.

When I was building my first house in 2014, I didn't want to spend more than $100,000. Building it from the ground up ended up costing me $160K, and I was *sick* about it. Fast-forward to now: we recently hired a designer to lay out the interior for our *new* home. The furniture and artwork alone cost over $100,000, and I was okay with that.

Circumstances change depending on your environment. If somebody told me back in 2014 that I would be spending six figures on furniture, I'd be like, *Absolutely not. Why would I do that?* As ambitious as I was, I just couldn't imagine it. My goal then was simply six figures by any means necessary.

I gave up a $200,000 salary in a pandemic. I ultimately parlayed that job into an even more lucrative contract position, but I had to deeply believe in myself to make the leap first. A lot of people making $200,000 are thinking *Man, this is the life.* Some people will even be making fifteen or twenty dollars an *hour* and they think they're living the life—I know, because once I was one of them! I had to broaden my horizons before I realized that even $200K was not the pinnacle for me.

At this point, I can practically respond to my students' objections in my sleep.

I don't have any money.
You can learn anything for free on the internet. Be willing to put in the time.

I don't have a college degree.
Neither do I. Suck it up, buttercup.

I'm not smart enough.
For most of my life, my GPA was lower than the price of a gallon of gas in the nineties.

I'm too busy.
We make time for what's important.

People aren't paying high salaries in my area.
If you get the skills and do remote work, you'll get paid plenty. It doesn't matter where you are.

I don't make enough money to pay for it.
Find another job. Upgrade your career!

Go after those excuses. And wherever you are, start moving forward. I've already cleared a lot of the obstacles. Now it's about pursuing one goal after another. This story's not over, because the journey never ends. There's always gonna be a next step, a next stage.

Before any of this happened, I had an idea of what my life was going to look like, all the way back to Rollerblading through Plano. When people don't recover from bad situations, it's because they don't have anything to look forward to, and that's usually because they never had a vision.

This book is especially for those people—the people in that same spot who don't have much hope. A lot of people in the places I grew up think they need to be entertainers, influencers, or drug dealers. You don't need to be famous to live a good life—it's just simply not the case. There are honest ways to take care of your family.

I grew up so freaking poor, and I just did not want to live like I did growing up. That was my motivation for everything. Any time I had the chance to get ahead, good or bad, I was going to take it. My ears always perked up at any opportunity.

I still haven't forgotten what's happened to me. Far from it. I've used it as fuel. You can either succumb to bad circumstances or you can take those experiences, learn from them, and transform them into the very thing that will propel you to the next level.

Tragedy taught me how to conduct myself in good times and bad. Now I know how to pull myself out of tough situations. I wanted a better life, and nothing was going to stop me: no person, no degree, not even me. I had to be relentless.

I'm just an ordinary guy that had to deal with adverse circumstances, but I persevered and ultimately made something out of myself. It's a cliché, but if I did it, so can you. Let's get it.

I want to leave a legacy of faith, generosity, and love, and I take daily action to bring that vision into reality. I feel so much fulfillment because I was intentional about my legacy, and I want you to feel the same way. It's never too early to think about how you want to be remembered. Write it out. How do you want to be remembered? What daily actions are you going to take to make it happen?

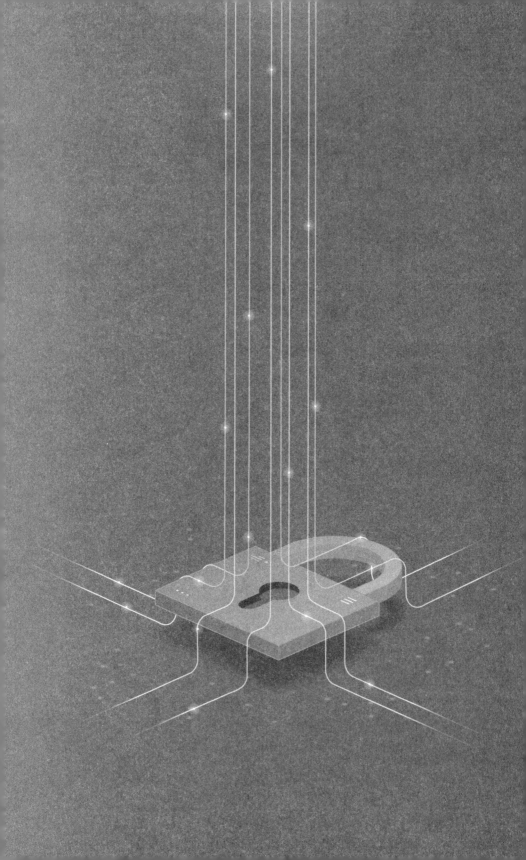

ABOUT THE AUTHOR

Boyd Clewis is the cofounder of Baxter Clewis Cybersecurity, the author of *Corporate Security: Proven Ways to Reduce Cybersecurity Breaches*, a member of the Forbes Technology Council, and a highly respected international expert and speaker on cybersecurity featured on *Forbes*, NBC, ABC, FOX, and CBS. He is dedicated to helping businesses implement effective security and compliance programs. He is trusted by many of the largest Fortune 500 companies; he plays a significant role in their cybersecurity initiatives.

He is regularly praised for his innovative and creative presentations for some of the world's leading cybersecurity conferences, including the PCI Community Meeting held in North America and Europe.

Through his consulting work, Boyd discovered the need for more diverse individuals in the cybersecurity space; therefore, he founded Baxter Clewis Cybersecurity, which has helped students land jobs at Google, Cisco, American Airlines, IBM, Honeywell, and more.